The Kids' Karate Book

The Kids' Karate Book

by Michael J. Dunphy, Ph.D.

Seventh–Degree Black Belt
and United States of America Karate Federation
All–American in Karate

Foreword by George E. Anderson
President, United States of America Karate Federation

Photographs by Joe Smithberger

WORKMAN PUBLISHING • NEW YORK

This book is dedicated to the memory of all the great teachers past and present, whose sacrifices and commitment have helped all of us find our way.

Text copyright © 1999 Wayne H. Kirn
Photographs copyright © 1999 Joe Smithberger

Library of Congress Cataloging-in-Publication Data
Dunphy, Michael J., 1957–
    The kids' karate book / by Michael J. Dunphy ; foreword by George E. Anderson ; photographs by Joe Smithberger.
        p. cm.
    Includes bibliographical references (p.)
    Summary: Introduces the basics of karate, discussing the techniques and uses of striking, kicking, and blocking, as well as karate legends, lore, and lingo. Includes a beginner's belt.
    ISBN 0-7611-1609-5
    1. Karate for children Juvenile literature.   [1. Karate]
I. Smithberger, Joe, 1962–   ill.   II. Title.
GV114.32.D86 1999 796.815'3—dc21   99-13138 CIP

Workman books are available at special discounts when purchased in bulk for premiums and sales promotions as well as for fund-raising or educational use. Special editions can also be created to specification. For details, contact the special sales director at the address below.

Workman Publishing Company, Inc.
708 Broadway, New York, New York 10003-9555

Belt manufactured in Pakistan
Book and package manufactured in the United States of America
First printing May 1999
10 9 8 7 6 5 4 3 2 1

Foreword

Kids are crazy about Karate. Over 50 million people study Karate worldwide, and it's estimated that more than half of them are kids. American children attend martial arts films in droves and regularly tune in to martial arts television shows.

In Karate competition, the largest divisions are the kids' divisions. Karate is recognized as a sport by the International Olympic Committee. Clearly, Karate has established itself as part of the mainstream of American kids' lives.

Parents of Karate kids enjoy their kids' Karate training as much as the kids do. They see how Karate helps to build character in their children through a synthesis of knowledge, physical courage and social responsibility. Karate kids—strong, bright and full of promise—develop an internal discipline that shines through as external calmness. And while young practitioners range from excellent natural athletes to kids working to overcome challenging disorders like hyperactivity or attention deficit disorder, in Karate any kid can participate and any kid can succeed.

In *The Kids' Karate Book,* Michael Dunphy presents important skills and drills in plain language accompanied by clear photographs. The exercises are direct and to the point, and, as the basic building blocks of Karate, are of great value to beginners and more advanced students as well. The drills are fun, but they are also serious exercises that should be approached with the utmost concentration. The USAKF is especially pleased that parents get a chance to assist kids in the drills, and we hope that parents will be supportive of all of their Karate kids' endeavors.

The National Coaching Staff of the USAKF recommends *The Kids' Karate Book* wholeheartedly to all aspiring Karate kids. There has been nothing like it published before!

George E. Anderson
10th Dan, Hanshi;
President, United States
of America Karate Federation;
Chairman, Central Tae Kwon Do Association;
Technical Director, U.S. Jujitsu Federation;
Director, Kwanmukan International,
Akron, Ohio

Contents

-Part 3-
Going Further

These are some of the real-life Karate kids who will show you all the right moves in this book.

Introduction
Using *The Kids' Karate Book*

If you're ready to begin your own journey toward mastering Karate, *The Kids' Karate Book* will tell you everything you need to know to get started.

How This Book Works

Part one, INTRODUCING KARATE, will tell you all about Karate's historical and geographical origins, plus the legends, lingo and lore of martial arts around the world. You'll also find out about the basics of training at home, and how to incorporate some essential elements of Karate—such as bowing and meditating—into your home training sessions.

After that comes the core of the book: part two, BASIC SKILLS, where all of the essential Karate stances, strikes, kicks and blocks are presented in a step-by-step format. These are the basic skills that you will carry with you wherever your journey in Karate leads.

At the end of each BASIC SKILLS chapter are the Power Drills. Power Drills are *super training:* they reinforce what you have learned about a skill and help you develop the coordination to perfect it. They're a lot of fun, and they're also a great way to share your training with the rest of your family or friends.

After each of the Power Drills sections, you'll find the USING KARATE IN YOUR LIFE pages. They'll clue you in to some of the personal values that can help turn a white belt beginner into a black belt master.

The white belt that comes with *The Kids' Karate Book* is a real Karate beginner's belt, so you can begin practicing *real* Karate right now. However, if you do decide you'd like to move on to advanced study someday, the information in part three, GOING FURTHER, will get you started. You'll learn how to choose a school, what advanced training is like and even more about the wide world of martial arts.

Two additional features mark your progress along the journey. THE KARATE CHOPS present fun facts, historical lore and martial arts trivia. WISE GUYS boxes record the words of real-life masters and great thinkers; true to the Karate spirit, their simple words express volumes of wisdom.

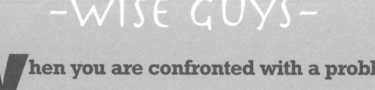

-WISE GUYS-

When you are confronted with a problem, a challenge, or an important decision, first of all be calm like the still water.

—Tadashi Nakamora,
Karate Technique and Spirit,
Shufunotomo Co. Ltd.,
Tokyo, 1986, 1993

Japanese and Korean Words

Throughout *The Kids' Karate Book* you'll see Japanese words, since modern Karate comes mostly from Japan, and Korean words, since Tae Kwon Do is from Korea. Both Japanese and Korean words can be found in the Glossary of Foreign Words on page 14. If you forget the meaning of a foreign word, just look it up in the glossary.

Safety First

As a white belt, you will be practicing *noncontact* Karate. This means that you cannot touch any person when you're practicing your Karate skills. In *The Kids' Karate Book,* skills are presented

in such a way that it is absolutely unnecessary to strike or kick someone else. That means *nobody,* including other students who may be using this book with you. Learning Karate is serious fun, but you can't leave out the serious part . . . fooling around with your skills on the street or in the hallway at school is not cool. If you ever decide to take a Karate class, the instructor there will teach you the very strict rules of contact Karate. Until then, use a target or a pillow—but never a real person—as the recipient of your strikes and kicks.

Now that you know what to expect, you can move into the heart of the book and learn all about Karate. Pay close attention, practice often, have fun, and let Karate enrich your life!

INTRODUCING KARATE

What Are Martial Arts?

Karate is one of the ancient martial arts. "Martial" comes from the name of Mars, the Roman god of war, and it means "having to do with war." In fact, every kind of martial art was originally created as a system of fighting or self-defense.

Over the years, martial arts masters refined their skills to the highest degree. Every movement seemed to be a work of art—like the brush strokes in a master-piece painting or the notes in a clas-sical symphony—and

Training and concentra-tion turn a basic karate skill into a work of art.

the masters themselves came to be called mar-tial artists.

There are dozens of dif-ferent kinds of martial arts.

-WISE GUYS-

A tree as big around as you can reach starts with a single acorn. The journey of a thousand miles begins with a single step.

—Lao-tzu, Chinese philosopher

Most of them originated in Asian countries, especially China, Japan and Korea; some of them have been practiced for centuries.

Karate

Karate is a Japanese word, and the correct way to say it is *kah rah*

The year 2000 summer Olympics in Sydney, Australia, mark Tae Kwon Do's first time as an official medal sport.

tay (not *kah rah tee)*. The word is usually translated as "empty hand," referring to the fact that a Karate practitioner holds no weapons in his hands.

The roots of Karate are complex. Influenced by ancient Chinese styles and developed into a system by Samurai warriors in Japan, a very effective form of empty-handed combat was brought to Okinawa, an island off the Japanese coast, in about 1,500 A.D. At that time the island was in a period of feudal confusion, with several warlords vying with one another for ultimate control. One clan named the Sho became very strong and tried to assert its authority by forbidding anyone but warriors to own a weapon.

The peasants of Okinawa were forced to find a way to defend themselves—with nothing but their own hands and feet. Blending traditional techniques from China and Japan with newer ideas from their own island, the "empty-handed" Okinawans fought back with the martial arts style that they named Karate.

During the early 1900s Karate was brought from Okinawa to mainland Japan. There it was further refined into the modern style that we practice today. From Japan, Karate spread to countries all over the world.

Tae Kwon Do

The Korean version of Karate is called Tae Kwon Do, which means "way of the foot and fist." Tae

KARATE CHOP

Hands Up

Originally, the word *Karate* was translated as "China hand." But during the early 20th century, when Karate was brought from the island of Okinawa to mainland Japan, a slight change was made in the characters that spelled the name China, and the word *Karate* was given a new meaning: "empty hand."

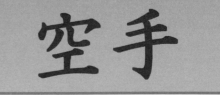

空手

3

Today, there are more than 30 million people studying Tae Kwon Do worldwide.

Kwon Do has been practiced for centuries, but became popular in the United States only in the 1960s.

Tae Kwon Do is known for its awesome kicks, especially high flying and jumping kicks. Many people consider the acrobatic kicking of modern Tae Kwon Do to be the most spectacular in the world of martial arts.

Tae Kwon Do is very similar to Japanese Karate, and the basic skills presented in this book apply to both styles.

Chinese Martial Arts

The Chinese martial arts are the oldest in the world. If you count all the regional styles, they number in the thousands. **Kung Fu** is the best known, but several

A painting of the Shaolin Temple, where martial arts were born.

other Chinese styles have gained recognition all over the world.

The Shaolin Temple, a Buddhist temple in the Hunan Province of China, is usually considered to be the true birthplace of martial arts. According to legend, in the year 520 a Buddhist monk named Bodhidharma visited the Shaolin monastery and was appalled to find that the monks there, who spent all their time meditating or translating books, were sadly out of shape and unable to defend themselves against bandits who might appear at any moment. Bodhidharma taught the monks a series of self-defense movements that came to be known as Kung Fu.

As time went on, the Shaolin monks became quite famous for

Modern-day Shaolin monks continue the rigorous training rituals established centuries ago by their predecessors.

their fighting abilities and the Shaolin Temple became a training center. People came from all over China to study martial arts there; even children as young as five were welcome, although they were expected to train almost all day, seven days a week.

Finally, the original Temple could not keep up with the demand for its teaching from China's population of fifty million, and several more Shaolin Temples were established in other parts of the huge country. The monks also traveled throughout the Far East, introducing their art to many different countries. There are still large martial arts festivals held at the Shaolin Temples each year.

Kung Fu is known all over the globe today, due in large part to the books and films of the great Bruce Lee, the world's most famous Kung Fu fighter.

The name Kung Fu may be interpreted many different ways, depending on how it's pronounced. Sometimes it means "human struggle," sometimes "special skill" and other times just "well done." Kung Fu masters

Disney's 1998 movie *Mulan* retells the Chinese legend of a young girl who uses Kung Fu to protect her father's honor.

KARATE CHOP

Legacy of a Master

The most acclaimed Chinese martial artist of all time is Bruce Lee, who was born in San Francisco but spent most of his youth in Hong Kong. A master in Kung Fu and several other martial arts, Bruce decided that traditional Kung Fu training was overly complicated, so he created his own system called Jeet Kune Do, or "the way of the intercepting fist." Bruce died at a very early age, but his many martial arts films have captured his legacy for the future.

believe that learning the correct body movements allows a student to make the most of his or her *chi*, the Chinese word for spirit or internal life force. The style has always been closely associated with Chinese philosophy, and many of its movements are inspired by animals or other aspects of the natural world. Some movements were even inspired by imaginary creatures from Chinese mythology, such as the dragon and the phoenix. Kung Fu is a vast and fascinating martial art.

Within the Kung Fu style there are hundreds of substyles. One unique substyle is **Wing Chun,** known for its incredibly rapid and relentless hand techniques. Trying to follow the handwork of Wing Chun masters can be dizzy-

Many Kung Fu moves are named for the animals they imitate, such as the white crane, the tiger and the leopard.

ing—their moves are so fast and furious that their hands literally become a blur.

The Chinese martial art known as **T'ai Chi,** whose name means "great ulti-mate fist," is practiced all over the world. T'ai Chi is a low-impact (actual-ly, no-impact) style that emphasizes relaxed and graceful exercises designed to promote health. Although it's practiced by students of all ages, T'ai Chi is especially popular among senior citizens, who believe it will help them live longer and remain healthy into advanced age.

KARATE CHOP

The Lion King, Karate Style

The traditional lion dance is part of the rich cultural heritage of China, and it has close associations with Kung Fu. Each Chinese village has its own papier-mâché "lion" that performs a special dance at festivals. The dancers who form the legs of the lion are usually members of the local Kung Fu club.

Unlike students of most other martial arts, T'ai Chi practitioners generally do not wear uniforms. They also do most of their training outdoors and can often be seen in parks doing hand and foot move-ments that resemble Karate movements in slow motion.

Japanese Martial Arts

The Japanese masters created many new styles of martial arts. Some characteristics of these styles, such as attention to the absolute perfection of even the simplest moves and the emphasis placed on the mental benefits of training, clearly reflect the inspiration of Japanese culture.

All "empty-handed" martial arts can be divided into two basic styles: striking (exemplified by

Judo competitors, locked in a take-down.

Karate) and grappling, which emphasizes wrestling techniques. The most famous grappling style is **Judo,** a Japanese sport whose name means "compliant way." Founded in Tokyo in 1882, Judo combines equal parts of physical education, self-defense and competitive sport. Judo introduced many new ideas to the martial arts world, including the traditional white uniform and the system of colored belts.

In Judo, competitors generally begin from a standing position and try to trip or throw their opponent. Points are awarded for clean throws and for holding a thrown opponent down on the mat.

Jujitsu is another Japanese grappling style. Its name means "gentle art" or "flexible art," and it teaches students to use their opponent's strength to their own advantage. Jujitsu is a more "no-holds-barred"

Next to Sumo wrestlers, most Western professional wrestlers would look small!

"Karate doesn't care if you're a boy or a girl. You can be your best anyway." —Sharon, age 10

style than Judo, since it includes more striking, kicking, locking, and even weapons techniques.

Sumo wrestling is the national sport of Japan. If you've ever seen Sumo wrestlers on TV (televised Sumo bouts are big business in Japan), you won't soon forget what they look like: huge, bearlike men (often tipping the scale at more than 400 pounds) wearing nothing but traditional loincloths so that opponents cannot grab each other by the uniform.

Sumo wrestlers fight inside a circular ring about 15 feet in diameter, and the object is to force an opponent to step outside the ring. Body charging, slapping, pushing, tripping and sheer strength are what Sumo is about.

KARATE CHOP

Female Warriors

Women have been an integral part of the martial arts movie business for decades. Early stars like Cynthia Rothrock and Karen Shepherd made movies both in America and in the Far East, but it was in Hong Kong movies that women really got a chance to shine. The first female superstar martial artist was Angela Mao, who costarred with Bruce Lee in *Enter the Dragon* in the early 1970s. More recently, *The Heroic Trio* starred the big three of Hong Kong cinema: Maggie Cheung, Anita Mui ("the Asian Madonna") and the amazingly agile Michelle Yeoh. This 1993 film is considered the classic expression of the fighting female.

At left: Superstar Michelle Yeoh.

The four most popular substyles of Japanese Karate are: Shotokan, Wado Ryu, Shito Ryu and Goju Ryu.

American movies have made much of **Ninjitsu,** a Japanese striking-style martial art whose name means "the art of stealth." The Ninja were clans of hired assassins who often killed their targets with poison or knives. They were such experts at camouflage and concealment that it was believed they had the power to make them-

Karate is a striking art that relies on punching and kicking rather than grappling.

selves invisible. Ninjitsu is a violent martial art that is best kept in the movies and out of real life.

Other Japanese striking styles include **Aikido,** a 50-year-old style that emphasizes flowing circular movements, and **Kendo,** the ancient art of sword fighting. (Modern students of Kendo wear armor and use bamboo swords so as not to actually hurt each other.) And finally we come to **Kobujutsu,** "the old warrior way," which incorporates various tools as striking weapons. It was used by common people who, unable to obtain traditional weapons, learned to defend themselves with ordinary agricultural tools such as threshing forks and rice flails. Kobujutsu may be a very ancient art, but recently it

KARATE CHOP

Shell Shock

Adapted from a comic book, the 1990 film *Teenage Mutant Ninja Turtles* was a spoof of traditional martial arts movies. The Turtles practiced Kobujutsu, and experts say it has some of the most authentic fight scenes of any Ninja movie ever made.

*In the 1600s, African slaves in Brazil created a colorful martial arts style called **Capoeira** (shown at right). Capoeira is very theatrical and is sometimes performed to music.*

has experienced an unexpected boost in popularity. The most famous fictional practitioners of Kobujutsu are the Teenage Mutant Ninja Turtles!

Martial Arts Around the World

Although China and Japan are the traditional homes of most martial arts, many interesting styles have evolved all over the globe.

Kali is the traditional self-defense style of the Philippines. Forced underground when the islands were conquered by the Spanish during the 16th century, the style survived and flourishes today.

Kali includes many unarmed techniques, but it is also famous for the use of sticks. It's said that when good Kali opponents meet, you can smell the smoke produced by the furious clash of their sticks.

Muay Thai kickboxing is the national martial art of Thailand. Kickboxing is somewhat like our Western boxing, but with fewer rounds. Fighters wear boxing gloves and footpads. Muay Thai has recently inspired countless kickboxing variants all around the world.

Another style, called **Kenpo,** was invented in Okinawa but fully developed in the United States during the 1940s by a Hawaiian native named Ed Parker. Kenpo is now considered an American style.

Kalaripayit, an ancient system from India, uses both unarmed and armed techniques. Its practitioners are known for their acrobatic flexibility.

Karate is a system of self-defense that does not require the use of weapons.

11

Becoming a Karate Kid

Every kid can be a Karate Kid. You don't have to be the best athlete in your class to learn Karate; you don't even have to be in great physical shape. It doesn't matter how tall you are, or how much you weigh, or how good you are at any other sport. You don't have to be the smartest kid in your class, and it doesn't matter if you're not one of the most popular kids in school. All you

The Japanese word for student is ka and someone who studies Karate is called Karate-ka.

need is an honest desire to learn Karate and the commitment to pursue your goal.

Karate is physical, active and intense, but all kids can advance and succeed if they stick to it

KARATE CHOP

Hard Hat Alert

You may have seen an exhibition of Karate masters breaking boards or bricks with their hands or even with their heads. Is it real? You bet. Breaking objects, which the Japanese call *Tamashiwara,* is a traditional part of Karate, but it is done only under the supervision of a highly qualified instructor. You should *not* try to do this on your own: you would almost certainly break your hand or a few fingers.

"I found a true extended family in Karate."
—Stephanie, age 16

-WISE GUYS-

To win one hundred victories in one hundred battles is not the greatest skill. To subdue the enemy without fighting is the highest skill.

—Chinese proverb

and give it their best. If, after reading the first section of this book, you decide that you *do* have the desire and *are* willing to make a commitment, you will already have earned the right to call yourself a "Karate-ka," or student.

People become Karate students for many different reasons. Some

people want to learn self-defense skills and develop the confidence that comes from knowing how to protect themselves or their family. Even though you may never have to use your Karate skills in real-life self-defense, Karate training will prepare you to handle a threatening situation if one should ever arise. You'll develop the clar-

ity of mind to talk your way out of danger (which is always the best way to handle a conflict) and you'll develop the quick reflexes needed to take advantage of an escape route (the second-best way to handle a conflict).

Other people learn Karate because it's a great sport. You can spend years improving your skills, yet you can start doing real Karate from the day you begin. It's a sport that has challenges tough enough for serious jocks, but it's also a sport in which you can set your own goals and work at your own pace.

If you enroll in a Karate class, you'll make new friends who share your enthusiasm for the art. At intermediate and advanced levels there are opportunities for competition, but even as a beginner you'll learn that this art is more about self-discovery than beating a competitor.

Physical fitness is one of the most popular reasons for entering the martial arts. Karate training is designed to improve your flexibility, strength, speed and endurance. A Karate training session is quite a workout, but you don't have to be in great shape to begin. If you work at your own pace and don't give up, it's likely that you'll soon be in much better shape than when you started!

No matter your reason for beginning Karate, you will soon discover that physical training is only one part of the story. Karate training is not just for your body; it's also for your mind and your spirit. Karate is a system of *self-perfection,* and that means becoming the best person you can be in every aspect of your life.

Important Karate and Tae Kwon Do Words

Japanese	Korean	Definition
dan	dan	a step or rank within black belt
do	do	way, method, path (of life)
dojo	do jang	martial arts school
gi (or dogi)	dobok	martial arts uniform
ka	jeja	student
kata	hyung	standard pattern of movements
kiai	kiap	the Karate shout; "spirit meeting"
kumite	daeryon	sparring
kyu	gup	grades below black belt
obi	ti	martial arts belt
rei	kyunggye	bow
sensei	sa bum	teacher
tatami	tatami	matted training area

Training the mind means developing the ability to think clearly and quickly. Training the spirit means developing values such as self-assurance, patience and discipline. "Discipline" is an especially important word in Karate, though this might at first

Dojo means school or training hall. In Japan they were modeled after traditional teahouses to include *tatami* (straw mats) and sliding rice paper walls.

seem strange to you; after all, you might associate the word with punishment or with being prohibited from what you want to do. But Karate students know that it means a lot more than that: discipline means setting your own goals and doing the things that move you closer to those goals.

Karate training can be tough, but most students agree that there are many benefits—sometimes even unexpected ones. For instance, some Karate Kids find that their training gives them an ability to focus that helps them perform better in school; others find that they can think and react more quickly, which makes them better at other sports like baseball or soccer.

Becoming a more confident person, a smarter student and a better athlete: these are big goals. But if you stick with your Karate training, you might find yourself able to reach more goals than you ever imagined. Karate training is all about doing your very best in every aspect of life.

—WISE GUYS—

What we see depends on what we look for.

—Japanese proverb

Karate asks you to train your mind and your spirit along with your body.

All About Karate Belts

The white belt that comes with *The Kids' Karate Book* is a lot more than just a way to keep your uniform closed: it is a very powerful symbol. A Karate belt, or *obi* (pronounced *oh bee*), is a visual representation of a student's level of achievement.

Karate masters know that the journey from white belt to black belt is long and hard, and that many students might get discouraged along the way. So they have created a series of ranks, or levels, for students to achieve as they progress.

Each rank is represented by different-colored belts. Each new color means that a student has

arrived at a higher level of achievement, and this reward for each small step makes the long road to black belt a lot more fun and manageable.

Think of these ranks as different grades in school; moving from

one rank to the next means learning new skills and improving upon what you've already learned.

Each rank in Karate has its own special belt color or stripe.

"Sensei always respects me, especially when I do my best." — Sean, age 9

KARATE CHOP

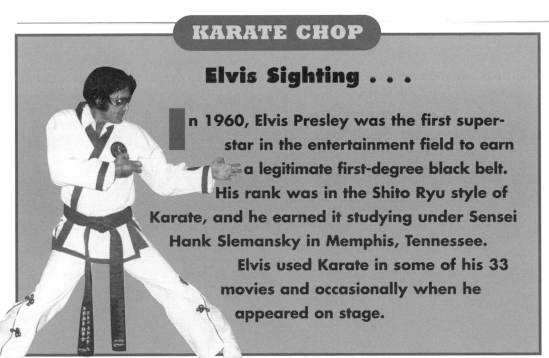

Elvis Sighting . . .

In 1960, Elvis Presley was the first super-star in the entertainment field to earn a legitimate first-degree black belt. His rank was in the Shito Ryu style of Karate, and he earned it studying under Sensei Hank Slemansky in Memphis, Tennessee. Elvis used Karate in some of his 33 movies and occasionally when he appeared on stage.

All students start their training as "white belts." Wearing the white belt signifies that you've taken the first step on the long road to success in Karate.

The process of earning a black belt in Karate starts with the white belt and moves in many steps over a period of several years. Of course, anybody can go to a martial arts supply store and purchase Karate belts in any color; but the real rank certificate that a colored belt comes with must be earned through dedicated practice and be given by a qualified instructor.

In Karate systems, there can be anywhere from 10 to 16 steps between white belt and black belt. The exact number of ranks and belts differs a little among various Karate schools and styles. One common ranking system uses this sequence: white, orange, yellow, blue, green, purple, brown, black.

Some schools also use stripes to indicate progress within each color rank. A stripe is usually a piece of red or white tape, about half an inch wide, that is placed near one end of the belt. Most schools award from one to three

—WISE GUYS—

In the beginner's mind there are many possibilities, but in the expert's mind there are few.

—Shunryu Suzuki, martial arts expert

stripes for each color, so a student may have a rank of "purple belt, third stripe," indicating that he or she is getting close to earning a belt in another color.

Since each style of Karate has its own system of colors, a student who is a blue belt in the Tae Kwon Do style of Chang Moo Kwon is not necessarily a blue belt in the Karate style of Goju Ryu. Likewise, the ranking systems of other forms of martial arts are not directly linked to those of Karate, so a student with a high rank in Karate might still be a lower rank in Judo or Jujitsu. This also means that many Karate students have two or more belts at the same time, depending on how many styles of martial arts they're studying.

How much time and effort will it take to advance? No two kids are exactly alike, so it's important to find the right routine for yourself. Devote enough time to training so that you keep advancing, but not so much time that you start falling behind in school or losing touch with your family and friends. To give you some idea of what to expect, it's likely that a hardworking student might train twice a week for two to four months in a Karate class before advancing from a white belt to the first colored belt.

In most Karate schools, students who are ready for advancement are required to demonstrate their skills in front of a panel of black-belt instructors. These examinations are meant to be a positive experience, and since students are not encouraged to try for the next step unless they're ready, most candidates are allowed to advance in rank. New belts are presented during class or at a special ceremony at the Karate school.

"I am working toward my black belt, and I'm getting better all the time." —Michael, age 7

To a beginner, it might look as if a black belt in Karate is the end of a long road, but in fact the real journey has just begun. In most martial arts there are at least 10 degrees, or levels, within the rank of black belt. In Karate, each degree of the black belt level is called a *dan* (pronounced like the name Don).

In order to earn the various *dan* grades, students must not only improve their Karate skills, but also meet minimum age requirements, study Karate for certain lengths of time, show loyalty to their teachers, and even teach others. The highest *dans* can sometimes take 50 years of Karate training to achieve.

KARATE CHOP

Ring Around the *Obi*

There's a curious and popular myth concerning the black belt. According to the myth, ancient Karate masters never washed their belts. A black belt was considered a sign of status because it suggested that the master's years of experience caused dirt to gradually change his belt from white to black.

In Karate you don't compete against your friends for belt ranks; you compete against yourself.

19

Gearing Up to Learn at Home

You don't need much gear to get started in Karate. For now, the most important thing is to wear comfortable, loose clothing that allows you to move freely. A large T-shirt or sweatshirt and a pair of loose-fitting lightweight gym pants should do fine.

A traditional Karate gi.

Make it a habit to use only clean clothes; a presentable uniform is a sign of respect for yourself, for Karate and, if you go further, for any future teachers, classmates or schools you might attend.

If you decide to enroll in a martial arts class, you will be required to buy a uniform called a *gi* (pronounced *gee,* with a hard "g"). A *gi* consists of a loose-fitting jacket and pants, something like a pair of pajamas. Karate students usually wear white *gis,* but students of other styles, such as Kung Fu, sometimes wear black ones.

The belt, or *obi,* is the most important part of the Karate uniform. Putting on your belt is a way of saying (to yourself and to anybody who may be instructing or helping you) that your training session is a very special time. While you're wearing your belt, you will be honoring your commitment to focus entirely upon your training and nothing else, and you will be reminded that you should not let any distractions get in the way.

Wear clothing that's casual and comfortable when you train, and don't forget to wear your obi!

Here's how to tie your Karate belt:

1 Unfold the belt and hold the middle of it in front of your belly button.

2 Wrap both ends of the belt around your back and cross them as shown.

3 Bring both ends of the belt to the front and lay the end in your right hand over the end in your left hand.

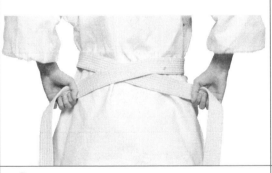

4 Tuck the end in your right hand under and behind both layers of the belt. Pull both ends tighter, keeping the two lengths even.

5 Bring the belt end in your right hand over the belt end in your left hand, and place it through the hole created by the crossed belt.

6 Tie a knot. When you're done, the knot should be in the middle and both ends should hang more or less evenly.

"I've learned that anything worthwhile can be learned with practice and dedication." —Cindy, age 12

Where to Practice

Where is the best spot in your home to do your training? You don't need much room; about 10 empty square feet will do fine. The family room or rec room is a good spot, if the rest of the family agrees to let you have it to yourself for a few hours each week. Your bedroom is okay, too, as long as you keep it clean and cleared of junk—a Karate-ka needs to have respect for his or her training area. If you live in a climate where it's warm all year round, there's no reason why you can't train outside, as long as it's a spot where you won't be disturbed.

If anyone in your family has an exercise mat, you might ask to borrow it; if not, choose a carpeted area or ask your folks if you can use an old area rug. Even though your first sessions will be very low-impact, you can still lose your balance in a stance and it's better to fall on a rug or mat!

Target Practice

As a white belt, you will be learning to punch and kick without making any contact with an opponent. But after you've mastered the moves of a basic strike or block, it might be useful to use a target in order to increase your accuracy.

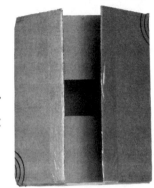

If you buy a commercial target, make sure to get one that's soft enough for beginners.

There are good commercial targets available for beginners. You can buy one at a *dojo* or at a martial arts supply store; they usually cost from $15 to $30.

Or, you can make your own safe target from materials that you probably already have at home. Use a simple cardboard box, approximately 12 by 4 by 10

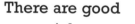

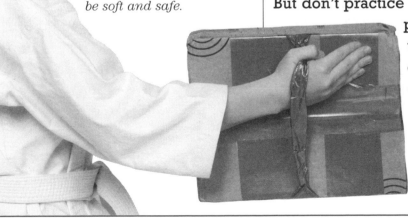

inches. Wrap the edges and corners of the box with a few layers of duct tape to make the box durable. Tap each corner of the box on a hard floor to flatten any sharp points.

To make a handle for your target box, layer two strips of duct

A homemade target should be soft and safe.

tape on top of each other around the width of the box. Leave the tape raised (unstuck) off one side of the box. Press the sticky side together by folding the tape in half, then wrap the folded tape with another piece of duct tape to form the non-sticky handle as shown. You might tape the box further on the edges for more strength.

When to Practice

When to train is really up to you. But don't practice in short time periods scattered throughout your busy day. Instead, schedule your practice for particular days of the week and at

Training Tip If you have long hair, tie it back so that it won't block your vision when you practice. Also, almost all forms of Karate require you to train in bare feet; as you practice basic skills you'll learn how to make your feet grip the floor as you progress. Be sure to keep your fingernails and toenails short, so your feet can grip the floor for better balance, and so you don't scratch anyone in practice.

a certain time of day. Try to do two or three training sessions each week, with each session lasting about an hour.

Your training sessions should not be done "on the run." A good session requires ample time for you to focus completely on your training.

23

Before You Train

Karate training is serious fun: there's no way you can do it without the right preparation. And since Karate is a discipline that's both physical and mental, it's necessary to prepare yourself in both respects. In other words, it's time to warm up your brain as well as your muscles! This section will show you how to

A Karate class always begins and ends with a bow.

get both your body and your mind in shape for the training ahead.

As you start, it's important to make your training sessions as "formal" as you can; act as if you were in a real class even though you're starting at home on your own. Give your sessions a structure,

with a distinct beginning, a middle and an end. Don't forget to follow up basic skills training with some Power Drills. Here's one way to structure a session:

- spend a few minutes meditating (you'll learn how on page 28)
- warm up
- learn a new basic skill
- review the basic skills you've already learned
- do some Power Drills

Most of all, remember that for a Karate-ka, every single training session is important.

Bowing

In most Asian cultures, people bow instead of shaking hands to greet each other. A bow means

In ancient Japan, Samurai warriors valued a peaceful mind as much as a powerful body.

"Hello" or "How do you do?" Westerners sometimes mistakenly think of bowing as a sign of servitude or inferiority, but in fact the bow is a sign of courtesy, not submission.

For Karate students, bowing takes on a slightly deeper meaning. When Karate students bow to each other, they're saying "Hello," but they're also saying "I respect the effort you are putting into your training, and I offer to train with you to the best of my ability."

Generally, students bow whenever they enter or leave the training floor of a Karate class. They also bow to their instructor and to other students. When you bow to another student who will possibly be a training partner, it is consid-

KARATE CHOP

Samurai Insurance Policy

The Samurai were aristocratic Japanese warriors who lived in Japan many centuries ago. They followed a code called "Bushido," in which their honor was worth more than their lives.

A Samurai warrior always wore his sword on the left side and drew the sword with his right hand. When he bowed, he would extend his left hand first, always keeping his opponent in sight. This way, he still would have been able to draw his sword with his right hand if need be.

So, to this day, the left hand is always extended first in a kneeling bow. It's a Samurai tradition.

ered correct to keep your eyes on him or her rather than lowering them; after all, a partner is also an opponent.

Even though you'll be training at home on your own, it's still a good idea to learn how to bow. You can practice your bowing when a friend or family member helps you with a Power Drill.

There are two basic kinds of Karate bows, and both of them are easy to learn.

The Standing Bow

The Standing Bow is the most common bow in Karate.

1 Stand with your arms hanging down, palms resting lightly at the sides of your legs; put your heels together so that your feet form a "V."

2 Keeping your back straight and your head still, slowly lean forward while you bend at the waist.

3 Pause briefly at the lowest point of the bow; don't let your head drop.

4 Return to the upright position and place your feet shoulder-width apart, pointing forward. Lightly close your fists.

The more you lower your head in a Standing Bow, the more respect you show.

The Kneeling Bow

More formal than the Standing Bow, the Kneeling Bow is usually performed at special ceremonies such as belt rank promotions.

1 Kneel down first on your left knee and then on your right knee, keeping your back straight.

"I like to bow to my friends and tell them that I learned about it in Karate." —Carli, age 7

Sit back so that your rear end rests on the back of your heels. The soles of your feet should be facing up with your right big toe crossed over your left big toe; or, you can also rest your weight on the balls of your feet with your toes pointing forward (whichever is more comfortable).

Place your hands flat on your thighs in front of you. In Japanese, this sitting position is called *seiza* (*say zah*).

Bowing symbolizes humility—an important value among all Karate-ka.

Now lean forward; as you do, put first your left hand and then your right hand down on the floor, pointing your fingers inward to form a "V."

Now lean forward and pause briefly at the lowest point of your bow, with your head about six inches above your hands.

Slowly start to straighten your back; as you do, put your right hand on your right thigh, and then your left hand on your left thigh.

Straighten your back completely and stand up.

KARATE CHOP

Name Game

In Japan and China, people list their last name first and their first name last. A title is generally put after someone's name instead of in front of it.

This means that if you were a Karate instructor named Billy Smith, you might be called Smith Teacher, or Smith Sensei.

"Connecting the mind, body and spirit is what Karate is all about." —Matt, age 14

KARATE CHOP

Make It Shine

Karate masters teach that unceasing repetition of the basic skills is necessary for improvement. In Karate the concept of repetitive daily practice is called *renma,* and the translation of this Japanese word combination is easy to remember: *it* means *"constant polishing."*

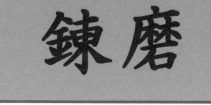

Meditating

Almost every style of martial arts from Asia includes some form of meditating as an essential part of practice. Meditation is a tried-and-true tool used to rid your mind of distractions and focus your energy on the task at hand.

Because not many people in the West do it, meditation may seem strange or even mysterious to you. But it's really very simple. Basically, meditating means sitting quietly and focusing only on what you want. In fact, in most Asian languages, the word for meditating may also be interpreted literally as "sitting."

Meditating has distinct physical benefits too, and once you learn how, you'll experience them with-in a few minutes after you begin. When you meditate, your breathing automatically becomes deeper and more regular. Your body relaxes—even more than when you're asleep! It's believed that such deep calm and relaxation makes you all the more alert and energetic when your meditation is over.

Meditating can be described as "emptying" the mind. A mind that has been emptied of all unimportant and unfocused thoughts has more room to concentrate on something important or new—like learning a Karate skill.

Some people have the notion that meditating in Karate is the same as practicing an Asian religion. Although meditation is used in many religions, including

Zen masters believe that a quiet mind can see things more clearly.

◖ KARATE CHOP ◗

The Beginning Never Ends

In Japanese, the word *shoshin* means "beginner's mind." It's thought that the mind of a child or a beginner is trusting and open to new ideas. Once the mind acquires knowledge, it begins to develop opinions and prejudices; in other words, it may gather more knowledge, but not necessarily more understanding.

A Karate-ka is encouraged to keep the spirit of *shoshin*, the beginner's mind, forever. In Karate the color white symbolizes the concept of beginning, and both the white belt worn by new students and the white uniform that they will still wear as experts are meant as reminders to maintain the beginner's mind.

Western ones such as Christianity, the meditation that Karate students practice is not a form of religion.

In many *dojo*, students meditate in a group just before class begins. Karate students believe that the few minutes of calm they experience during a brief meditation will increase their energy for the session that follows.

You can meditate standing, sitting, kneeling, or lying flat on your back. Each *dojo* has its own system of meditation (in some *dojo*, students meditate before and after class; in others, there is no meditation at all). No matter which way it's done, Karate-ka draw strength and focus from the silence of meditation. It's like the calm before the storm!

The Mountain in Your Mind

If you'd like to try meditating at home, here's a simple method you can use on your own:

1 Find a spot where you're not likely to be disturbed for a little while (your bedroom is probably a good place).

2 Kneel comfortably or sit in a cross-legged position; keep your back straight.

3 Close your eyes partially or completely.

4 Breathe slowly; inhale through your nose and exhale through your mouth. At the beginning of your meditation, try holding your breath for a few seconds.

5 Imagine a single large object in nature, like a tree or a mountain or waves crashing on the beach; try to think only of that image.

6 Every time you realize that your mind has wandered away from the image, gently refocus it; don't worry if at first your mind seems to wander all over the place. Just remember to gently bring it back to the image you chose.

You're not really supposed to nap during meditation, but don't worry if you do fall asleep; just finish your meditation when you wake up.

How long you meditate is up to you. But you'll probably find that even a few minutes before each training session will make a big difference in your ability to focus.

Once you've learned what a useful tool meditation can be, don't be surprised if you find yourself using it in your life outside the training room. For instance, you might do a brief meditation in order to clear your mind of distractions before an exam, or to muster up maximum energy before a swim meet, or even to get you through one of life's unavoidable stressful moments—like a visit to the dentist!

The masters describe Karate as "moving mediation." They are referring to the intense concentration and awareness that a student strives for in training.

Karate Breathing

You probably consider breathing to be something that comes naturally; after all, you hardly ever think about breathing but you do it all the time. In fact, breathing is one of the functions that the body performs automatically, without you having to think about it.

As a Karate-ka, however, you will learn how to make the most out of every single breath you take! And learning to breathe properly can help you move faster, think more clearly and strike harder.

Karate students practice breathing as part of their training, and they consider proper breathing a physical skill. In general, when a move requires drawing your arms or legs into your body, as in chambering (see page 54), you should inhale. When you push or thrust your arms or legs away from you, as in striking or kicking, you should exhale. The more fully you exhale, the stronger your strike will be.

Although most of us normally breathe in and out through our mouths, when extra energy is needed it's actually better to breathe *in through the nose* and *out through the mouth.* The mucus and small hairs in the nasal passages help clean the air and warm it before it goes into the lungs.

Try taking a deep breath through your nose. Take your time (most of us breathe too often and too shallowly). Draw the breath down as though the air is going into your stomach, and when you feel full, hold the air for a moment. Now tighten your stomach muscles slightly and breathe smoothly out through your mouth. You have begun your practice of Karate breathing.

Karate-ka always remember to breathe slowly and deeply.

"It's really cool to wear my Karate suit and scream."
— Kristie, age 5

Shout About It: The Kiai

One of the best ways for a beginner to remember to breathe properly is to learn to do a real Karate shout. In Japanese Karate, the shout is called the *kiai* (pronounced *key eye*). In Korean Tae Kwon Do, it's called the *kiap* (pronounced *key ap*). Both words mean "spirited yell" or "spirit meeting."

If you get into the habit of doing a loud *kiai* when you execute a strike or kick, you can't help but breathe out correctly. The act of shouting also stimulates your body energy and your spirit.

To do the *kiai,* yell out the English word "eye." Your shout should be quick and sharp, never long and slow. It is meant to be done during a strike, kick or block when your arm or leg is fully extended.

As you learn some of the strikes and kicks in the next section, practice doing them with the *kiai.* You'll be amazed at the extra power and focus the shout will help you find.

To make your kiai *more effective, exhale completely as you shout.*

Choose Your Path

The Chinese word *do* (pronounced *doe*) is used frequently in many martial arts. Literally, *do* means "way" or "method of procedure." But in Karate and Tae Kwon Do it also means "chosen path." A student who has chosen *Karate-do* has made a commitment that Karate will be an essential part of his or her own path through life.

Warming Up

Before you do any kind of sport, you should do a short warm-up. Warming up gets your heart pumping faster and loosens up your muscles to help prevent muscle and joint injuries; it also helps you perform better. A warm-up for Karate or Tae Kwon Do involves moving the major joints (neck, shoulders, hips, knees and ankles); stretching the muscles, especially the ones you use for training; and increasing your heart rate so that the blood circulates more freely.

The eight-step warm-up routine shown on the next three pages is easy to follow on your own, and it gets the job done in a short time. You should do each of these exercises before you begin practicing your Karate skills.

❶ Who's on First?

Stand in a relaxed posture with your feet shoulder-width apart. Look up at the ceiling and then down at your feet five times. Turn your head and look to your left five times. Then look to the right five times.

In the High Roller, first cross your arms and then roll them like wheels.

❷ High Roller

Roll your shoulders five times. Reach your arms up above your head as high as you can, and then drop your arms to your sides.

Cross your arms in front of you. Then, uncross them and drop them back down to your sides. Now, make large circles with your arms, rolling them in one direction and then in the other, as if your arms were spokes on big bike wheels. Do this five times.

● Hula Hips

Put your hands on your hips and keep your back straight, your head still and your feet flat on the floor. Circle your hips all the way around five times to the right and then five times to the left (as if you were using a hula hoop).

-WISE GUYS-

Do not seek to follow in the footsteps of the wise. Seek what they sought.

—Basho

4 Knees in Orbit

Put your feet and your knees close together. Bend your knees and put your hands on top of your knees (right hand on right knee, left hand on left knee). Gently circle your knees all the way around to the right five times and then to the left five times.

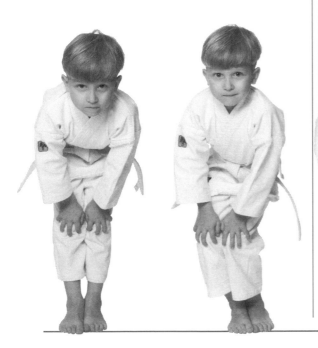

Counting to Ten

Learning to count in the language spoken by the original masters of the martial art you're studying can be fun—and it can make your Karate training feel more "real." Warm-up is a great time to practice counting. If you're learning Japanese-style Karate, you'll want to count in Japanese; if you're doing Tae Kwon Do, you'll want to use the Korean words.

English	Japanese	Korean
one	*ichi*	*hana*
two	*ni*	*dool*
three	*san*	*set*
four	*shi* (or *yon*)	*net*
five	*go*	*da sot*
six	*roku*	*yo sot*
seven	*shichi* (or *nana*)	*il kop*
eight	*hachi*	*yo dol*
nine	*ku*	*a hop*
ten	*ju*	*yol*

Stretching before training will help you avoid injuries and pulled muscles. But a few minutes of stretching after your workout, when your muscles are all warmed up, will really maximize your flexibility.

5 Reach for the Sky

Keeping your fleet flat on the floor, reach your arms as high as you can above your head, push your belly forward, and inhale. Then exhale as you bend over with your knees straight. Let your arms hang down toward the floor for about five seconds. (Don't bounce.)

6 Step It Up

Place your feet shoulder-width apart. Take a long step forward with your right foot as you roll up onto the ball of your left foot (the bottom front of the foot). Your right foot should remain flat on the floor with your right knee bent; don't extend your knee beyond your toes. Keep your back straight and press your stomach forward. Hold the position for five seconds; you should feel a gentle pull on your left leg. Repeat the stretch with your left foot forward.

7 Backseat Driver

Sit on the floor with your feet straight out in front of you, about six inches apart. Inhale and then exhale as you reach out toward your feet with your hands. Let your head drop down and reach as far as you can until you feel tightness in the back of your legs. Hold this position. (Don't bounce.) Do this five times.

8 The Bounce Counts

Stand up and place your feet shoulder-width apart. Bounce up and down for two to three minutes to speed up your heart rate a little.

Now you're ready to practice some real Karate moves!

Listen to your body. Some days it may be telling you that, for whatever reason, you are simply too tired or too tight to train the way you want to. On those days, take a break or take it slow.

-PART 2-
BASIC SKILLS

Time to Begin

In this part of the book, it's okay to skip from section to section: you might decide to learn the first strike, the Forefist, and then move on to the first kick, the Front Kick, before you learn more strikes. But you should learn the skills *within* each section in the order in which they are presented; that is, be sure to learn the first block, the High Block, before you try any other block.

Karate skills can be more easily learned when they're broken down into basic steps. As you learn each skill, think about the parts that make up the whole and try to get each part just right.

Practice the steps of each skill one at a time. Slowly repeat each one over and over again, and then check the illustrations in this book from time to time to make sure you remember accurately what the movement is supposed to look like. After you've practiced each part many times, put them together in sequence.

At first you may find that you have trouble maintaining your balance as you slowly go through the steps of a skill. Later, as you speed up the sequence, balance becomes easier but hitting your target becomes more difficult. With practice (a lot of it!) you will develop strength, better balance and keener accuracy.

Of course, after you've learned a skill correctly, the time will come when you don't have to think about its separate parts.

All your training sessions will pay off as all the steps of a skill blend together into the kind of quick, powerful and seamless skill for which Karate is famous.

Picture yourself talking with Mark McGwire and Sammy Sosa, two of the greatest home run hitters in the history of major league

Muscles have memory, so once you finally learn a skill it's likely that you'll never forget it.

baseball. If you asked them how you could become good enough to play on a major league team, they would very likely tell you to start with the basic skills of baseball—and to get ready for many hours of practice.

Chances are that basketball's Michael Jordan, golf great Tiger Woods, and tennis star Venus Williams would agree. The best athletes in the world practice the basic skills of their sport over and over again. Even pros never quit studying the basics.

As much as any other art, or maybe even more, Karate depends on learning basic skills and practicing them repeatedly. It's not unusual for advanced students to realize that they've never done a basic skill totally correctly, even though they've practiced it hundreds or thousands of times! There's no getting around it: if you want to start on the path to excellence in Karate, you've got to stick with the basics.

-WISE GUYS-

When we apply our Karate well, nothing is wasted and nothing is withheld.

—George E. Anderson
American Martial Arts Expert
President, USAKF

Custom dictates that Karate-ka always leave their shoes at the edge of the tatami *when they train.*

STANCES

There's an old proverb that says you must learn to walk before you can run. Well, in Karate, you must learn to stand before you can move.

Stances are the key to good Karate form. A stance is just what it sounds like—a way of standing—but it is also a position of readiness.

Stances do have some use in self-defense, but for beginners they are more training tools than actual moves. Their role in your own Karate training is to help you develop balance and to get you into the habit of being ready for anything. Stances also exercise the large muscles of your legs and build up your leg strength.

Most styles of Karate and Tae Kwon Do use five or six basic stances, plus a number of advanced ones. The six basic stances presented in this section are very important, since each one prepares the Karate-ka to be ready for different kinds of challenges from opponents.

In addition, each stance provides a different kind of exercise for your legs, knees, ankles and hips.

Karate-ka in dojo *classes always stretch before they practice their stances.*

IN THIS SECTION:

Skills
Front Stance
Back Stance
Horse Riding Stance
Sumo Stance
Cat Stance
Cross Stance

Front Stance, viewed from the side.

Front Stance

Zenkutsu Dachi
(zen koot soo dah chee)

The first stance taught in Karate is usually the Front Stance, which can be done in one of two ways: the left Front Stance or the right Front Stance.

To get into a left Front Stance, stand up and place your feet shoulder-width apart with your toes pointing straight in front of you. Put your hands on your hips. Step forward with your left foot about twice the distance of your normal walking step.

How to Do It

Bend your left knee so that it lines up over the top of your left foot. Your right knee should be just slightly bent. Let your hips relax and try to imagine your center of gravity, where your body is heaviest, being below your waist. Be sure your back is straight, and keep both heels on the floor.

Stand in this position with your left knee bent out over your left foot for one minute. This stance places your body weight slightly forward so that you feel more pressure on your front leg. You should be able to feel the muscles in your left thigh tightening, then starting to tire: when you feel your muscles starting to ache, it's time to stop.

Now try a right Front Stance. It's the same position, but with the right leg forward instead of the left leg.

After you've learned the Front Stance, ask a friend or family member to time your stance. If you can hold it for two minutes, you're doing very well for a beginner. Increase the time gradually until you can hold the stance for five minutes.

Once you've mastered this stance, you can do exercises while you hold your position. For instance, try bending and stretching your ankles—this helps to develop your kicking strength and your ability to move your foot quickly. Switch legs often to develop both equally.

Back Stance

Kokutsu Dachi
(koh koot soo dah chee)

The Back Stance is used in Karate almost as often as the Front Stance, but it's actually a more challenging stance to master. The Back Stance requires you to place much more weight on one leg than on the other, and to hold your body sideways.

Just like the Front Stance, the Back Stance can be done with either the right or left foot supporting your weight.

How to Do It

Stand up straight and place your feet side by side, pointing straight ahead. Turn your head all the way to your left. Keeping your chest facing front, point your left foot in the direction you are looking. Your feet should form a right angle. Step your left leg out about two feet as you place your weight down on your right leg.

Your right knee should be bent out over your right foot, and your left knee should be slightly bent as well. As in the Front Stance, keep your back straight and keep both heels on the floor. You should have about 70 percent of your weight on your back (right) leg.

Hold your hands open or in the "Sword" position (see pages 60–61). Keep your right arm close to your body, with your elbow pressed against your side and your hand just in front of your belly. (Your right arm is now in the "chamber" position; you'll learn more about chambering and also about making a good Karate fist in the section on strikes.) Extend your left arm forward, as if you were going to strike a target but stopped halfway there.

Now try to do the same stance with  your right leg out to the side. Karate students always practice on both sides in order to develop balanced muscle strength.

Back Stance, rear view.

Horse Riding Stance

Kiba Dachi
(kee bah dah chee)

The Horse Riding Stance is one of the two most common "straddle" stances, which help you strengthen your thigh muscles and increase the flexibility of your hips and ankles.

Try to hold the Horse Riding Stance for as long as five minutes with your knees bent as deeply as possible. You'll quickly understand why Karate students develop strong legs.

How to Do It

Stand up straight and place your feet shoulder-width apart, with your toes pointing straight in front of you. Now move both of your feet directly sideways about 12 inches, keeping your toes pointed forward. Make fists with both hands. Hold both arms very close to your body, with your elbows pressed against your sides and your fists facing forward.

Keep your back straight, and bend your knees as far as you can without allowing your rear end to poke out behind you. Push your knees outward toward your feet. The position you've assumed is very similar to that of a person riding a horse.

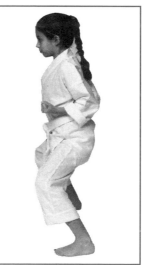

Horse Stance, side view.

Sumo Stance

Shiko Dachi
(shee koh dah chee)

Another common "straddle" stance is the Sumo Stance, which is similar to the Horse Riding Stance except that your feet and knees are tilted outward at a 45-degree angle.

Don't make fists with your hands; instead, keep them open, palms facing down. Hold your palms a few inches above your knees. Again, work up to holding the stance for five minutes.

KARATE CHOP

Classic Karate Clips

Some of Bruce Lee's greatest movie scenes are now available on video: Lee's screen test for *The Green Hornet*, in which he demonstrates traditional Kung Fu moves and shows his lightning-fast speed and perfect control; his battle with Chuck Norris in the Roman Colosseum in *Return of the Dragon;* and the final scenes of his last film, *Game of Death*. (The last twenty minutes feature Bruce in great fight scenes, including one with Kareem Abdul-Jabbar).

Cat Stance

Neko Ashi Dachi
(neh koh ah shee dah chee)

A frightened cat will arch its back, draw in its front paws and place all of its weight on its back feet. This posture keeps the cat's front paws free to defend against an attacker.

The Cat Stance is a position of readiness that resembles a cat in self-defense mode. In this stance, almost all of your weight is placed on one leg; the other leg is tucked in very tightly just in front of you.

How to Do It

Place your heels together with your toes angled outward at 45 degrees. Place all your weight on your right leg and put your left foot on its ball (the front part of the underside of your foot) about eight inches in front of your right heel. Keep your back straight and bend both knees.

Make fists with both hands and hold your right elbow close to your side. Hold your left forearm (the area between your elbow and your wrist) at a 45-degree angle to your body, with the knuckles of your fingers facing your chest.

Cat Stance, side view.

Cross Stance

Kosa Dachi
(koh sah dah chee)

A Karate-ka in a Cross Stance might appear to have very little balance and almost no capability for movement. But in fact the Cross Stance, when done properly, will allow you to move and turn very quickly in a variety of self-defense techniques.

How to Do It

The Cross Stance is formed by crossing one leg either *in front of* or *behind* the other.

Stand up straight with your feet shoulder-width apart, your toes pointing forward and both hands on your hips. Slide your left leg behind your right leg so that your right foot is flat on the floor and your left foot is up on its ball. Bend your knees and allow yourself to drop slightly downward. When you've moved into the stance, your feet should still be about shoulder-width apart.

The important thing to remember is that you must allow your legs the space in which to cross. If you feel that your legs are too tightly wrapped or that you have no balance and are about to trip yourself, you haven't allowed enough space for your legs to pass each other.

The Cross Stance allows you to react quickly; it can be used in advanced self-defense to trap an opponent's leg in the "X" formed by your own legs, to brace yourself for turning kicks or to evade a powerful incoming blow.

Like the other stances, the Cross Stance builds leg strength and ankle flexibility, which will pay off when you get into Karate kicking.

Cross Stance, rear view.

Karate Commitment:

Giving Your All

Making a commitment means making a promise and sticking to it. As a student of Karate, you are encouraged to make and honor commitments as part of your training. Every time you tie on your belt, you make a promise to work at improving your Karate skills. When you bow to a partner before training, you make a promise to give the session your best effort. Even earning a new color belt in Karate means making a new commitment; while you're being rewarded for com-pleting the requirements of one rank, you're also making a promise to learn what is required in the next rank.

The most important commitment you will make in Karate is the promise to practice to the very best of your ability. It's a long-term promise—for many years or possibly for the rest of your life—and it means giving your training your all.

What exactly does it mean to give your all? Should you train every afternoon and night after school instead of doing your homework? Should you quit playing another sport or spending time with your friends so that you have more time for Karate? No way.

Karate is about developing your full potential and pushing the limits. Turning your whole life over to Karate is not necessary; leading a healthy life that enables you to focus and to do your best when you *are* training is what's required. Students who do nothing but train limit themselves in a lot of ways.

Karate commitment means more than just perfecting your physical skills. It means building strength in three areas: body, mind and spirit. A Karate-ka excels only when all three are in balance.

Building a strong body is the easiest part to understand—it's obvious that unless your body is in good shape you'll have a tough

> **"I like karate because I can do a lot of fun stuff *and* reach my goals."** —Chris, age 9

time with the more rigorous training of advanced Karate. Staying in shape means getting enough rest and healthy food, and steering clear of substances that weaken the body, such as drugs and cigarettes.

The second part of Karate commitment is strengthening the mind. Karate is just as much a mental activity as a physical one. For example, a top Karate competitor who has perfected many advanced-level punches and kicks cannot be a winner without knowing the best moments to use them.

Spirit, the third part of Karate commitment, may be the most important. Spirit means staying enthusiastic through many hours of tough and repetitive practice. It also means using your skills for the right reasons.

Since you're just beginning, it could be pretty easy to let your commitment burn out or to lose sight of your goal. But it's a lot easier for a white belt to focus on earning the first color belt (probably orange) than to dwell on how far it is to the black belt. Like mile markers in a marathon race, belt ranks are interim goals that will encourage you to keep going.

Keeping a commitment can be tough, but the rewards make it worthwhile. Have you ever noticed that people who are physically fit, strong-minded and strong in spirit tend to be happier and more successful in everything they do?

There's one more reward that's worth thinking about: the benefits of being trustworthy and reliable. Honoring the commitments you make in your daily life will earn you the trust of your family and friends.

-WISE GUYS-

To hear is to forget, to see is to remember, to do is to understand.

—Chinese proverb

STRIKES

In Karate, the word "strike" may refer to any offensive move, including both hand and foot techniques. But in common practice, "strike" usually refers to a hand technique; foot techniques are called kicks. The word "punch" is also used frequently, but in fact only one hand technique—the Forefist—is properly called a punch.

Drawing on the groundwork of skills you have already learned—extra energy from the *kiai* and Karate breathing, flexibility and endurance from good warm-ups, balance and focus from your stances—you can learn how to turn your own Karate strike into a powerful force.

Karate strikes can be divided into two basic types: closed-hand and open-hand. Within these two basic types are many variations, named according to hand position. This section will explain six of the most common strikes: three open-hand strikes and three closed-hand.

Ready, Set, *Strike!*

The starting position for all six basic strikes is the same: stand with your feet shoulder-width apart and your hands hanging down at your sides. Then take a small step forward with your right foot just for balance.

After you complete each strike, you should return to the starting position.

IN THIS SECTION:

Skills
Forefist Punch
Backfist Strike
Hammerfist Strike
Sword Hand Strike
Palm Heel Strike
Ridge Hand Strike

Striking Power Drills
The News-Breaking Drill
Crack the Whip
The Jackhammer

Forefist Punch.

Any strike may be done with either your right or your left hand. The instructions in this section illustrate only one way (right- or left-handed striking), but you should practice each strike with *both* the right and the left hand.

After you can do each step of a strike smoothly, try the strike using your soft target.

Striking Terms

Learning a few other Karate terms at this point will help you make the most of the Basic Skills section.

The word *chamber* refers to the position you take just prior to delivering a strike or a kick. To understand the chamber position picture a tiger crouched down low with its limbs pulled in close to its body, just before it pounces. Most skills require you to chamber either your arm or your leg, and sometimes both.

Extension refers to the position in which your striking hand or foot is at its farthest reach. When you're using a soft target to practice a strike, for example, the moment of impact occurs just before full extension.

A *thrust* is a fast movement of your arm or leg, usually directly forward or backward; it is designed for maximum impact. The first strike you will learn, the Forefist, uses a thrusting technique.

A *sweep* is a broad, smooth movement of your arm or leg, usually sideways. The Backfist Strike may be done as a sweep.

A *snap* is a very fast, whiplike delivery of a strike or kick. It is usually followed immediately by a quick rechambering of the striking hand or foot. Generally, a snapping technique does not end in full extension, since a very strong snap could put too much pressure on the elbows or knees. Karate-ka develop control of their muscles so that they are able to execute a snap exactly when and to what extent they want to. Think of a snap as the last burst of energy you give to a strike.

Striking surface refers to the area on your hand or foot that actually makes contact with a target during a strike.

HOW TO MAKE A KARATE FIST

The three most common closed-hand Karate strikes are the Forefist, the Backfist and the Hammerfist. Each of these strikes requires that you learn how to form a proper fist.

After you can form a good fist, you'll learn how to use different parts of the fist for different strikes.

1 Wrap all four of your fingers inward with all of your fingernails tucked into your palm and hidden from view.

2 Wrap your thumb over the outside and across your index and middle fingers, just under the second knuckle of each.

3 Squeeze your fist tightly. Keep the back of your fist level with your forearm.

Forefist Punch

Zuki
(zoo kee)

The Forefist is the one closed-hand Karate strike that is more properly called a punch. You'll use this strike more than any other, so it's important to get every part right. The twisting action of your fist and arm is what helps to increase the speed and energy transfer at impact.

When you practice the punch, notice how both arms move at the same time; one delivers the punch and the other pulls into your hip.

The instructions will lead you through a right-handed Forefist Punch.

STRIKING SURFACE: the big knuckles of your index finger and middle finger

How to Do It

➊ Chamber.

Stand with your feet shoulder-width apart and your left foot one step in front of your right. Close both hands into fists. Tuck your right upper arm and elbow against your right side. Press your right fist against your side just above your belt, with your thumb knuckle pointing away from you (chambered position).

Extend your left arm straight out from your shoulder. Your left fist should be chest-high, with its thumb knuckle pointing to your right. Take in one full breath through your nose, and keep your shoulders relaxed.

➋ Push and pull.

In one smooth motion, push your right fist forward and pull your left fist back, keeping your arms tucked into your sides. Begin to exhale through your mouth, and remember to keep your shoulders relaxed.

● Twist your fists.

As your fists pass each other in front of your chest, begin to twist them so that both thumb knuckles are moving counterclockwise (to your left). Do not twist your shoulders; they should be straight. Keep your elbows close to your body.

● Snap and shout.

Keep extending your right arm outward and pulling your left arm close against your left side into the chambered position. (Note that this strike begins with the right arm chambered, but ends with the left arm chambered.) Keep breathing out.

Your right fist should be facing down; your left fist should be facing up. Now snap your right wrist into full extension and shout "Eye!" (the *kiai*).

● Rechamber.

Pull your right arm back into the chambered position. Extend your left fist straight out at chest height. As you do, twist both fists clockwise to the right. This is the same position as in Step 1.

Repeat the punch and try to blend all five movements into a smooth sequence. Now try a left-handed Forefist Punch.

Backfist Strike

Uraken
(ooh rah ken)

Imagine that an annoying fly is buzzing around your head. Swat at the imaginary fly with the back of your hand. Now do the same thing with your fist closed. The closed-hand Backfist Strike is like a powerful swat.

As it was for the Forefist Punch, the key to a good Backfist is the twisting action of your arm and fist. Begin practicing slowly and without power; later, speed it up and give it some snap.

The instructions will lead you through a left-handed Backfist; be sure to practice the strike with your right hand as well.

STRIKING SURFACE: the big knuckles of your index finger and middle finger

How to Do It

❶ Chamber.

Begin in the same starting position you used for the Forefist Punch: feet shoulder-width apart, left foot one step in front of the right. Make Karate fists with both hands.

Raise your left arm up so it is straight out in front of you with your fist closed and your left thumb knuckle pointing to your right. Place your right arm across the front of your chest so that your closed right fist is touching your left shoulder. Your right elbow should be pointing forward.

❷ Extend and pull.

Now straighten your right arm directly out in front of you at shoulder height. As you straighten your right arm, twist your right fist so that your thumb is pointing up to the ceiling. At the same time, pull your left arm back to the chambered position on your left side.

At first, try to make a gentle sweeping action with your fist. Later, as you practice and improve, change your sweeping action into a faster whipping action, or snap.

❸ Snap and shout.

Snap your left arm into full extension and give a *kiai*. Your elbow should be completely straightened out at this point.

❹ Rechamber.

Pull your right arm back to the position it was in for Step 1.

Repeat the steps several times. Then try reversing the directions for a left-handed Backfist Strike. Don't forget to give a good *kiai*.

Training Tip
Remember, a good Backfist is quick and snappy!

KARATE CHOP

Let's Get Physical

Instructors say that Karate is 10 percent physical and 90 percent mental. That's because, much more than in weight training or aerobic exercise, you must put intense concentration into each movement you make.

Hammerfist Strike

Kentsui
(ken zoo ee)

The closed-hand Hammerfist Strike is easy to picture: pretend you're a judge in a court of law and pound your gavel!

Just like a real hammer, the Hammerfist can sweep straight down or sideways. This strike is the simplest of all the hand techniques.

STRIKING SURFACE:
the "meatiest" part of your hand, opposite your thumb between your wrist and your pinkie

How to Do It

❶ Lift the Hammer.

Begin in the same starting position you used for the Forefist and Backfist strikes: feet shoulder-width apart, the left foot one step in front of the right. Make Karate fists with both hands.

Lift your left arm straight out in front of you so your left fist is shoulder-high and your left thumb knuckle points to your right. Place your right arm next to your head with your elbow bent so your right thumb is about four inches from your right ear. Your right elbow should point up and away to your right.

❷ Lower the Hammer.

Begin to bring your right fist down with a slight twisting motion so your right thumb knuckle is facing the ceiling. At the same time, begin pulling and twisting your left arm into chambered position at your left side.

❸ Slam the Hammer.

Stop your right fist at about the height of your belt, and at the same time fully chamber your left arm. Both fists should snap at the moment your arms stop moving; give a loud *kiai* at that moment.

Once you've learned the steps of the Hammerfist, do Steps 2 and 3 at the same time. Practice the strike with your left fist as the hammer. Then try the Hammerfist with your soft target.

Training Tip Friends who understand Karate won't think you're vain if you practice in front of a mirror. It's a great way to be certain you're doing things right. Before you begin, make sure that even at full extension your strikes or kicks will land several inches away from the mirror.

KARATE CHOP

Get Smart . . . Get Away

The first rule of self-defense is to stay alert. You should always be aware of danger; but even more important, you should scope out an escape route and be ready to flee as soon as possible.

A Karate technique is considered successful if it gives you just enough time—a "window"—in which to make your escape.

Sword Hand Strike ("Karate Chop")

Shuto
(shoo toh)

Get ready for something really awesome! You've probably seen this strike many times before—in movies or tournaments—but you might not have known you were watching a Sword Hand because it's so often called a "karate chop." For many people, the blazing speed and power of this strike have become synonymous with Karate itself.

When you do the Sword Hand Strike, notice how the palm of your hand is extended, your wrist lines up with your forearm, and your thumb is tucked alongside your hand.

STRIKING SURFACE: the "meaty" area of your hand between your wrist and the beginning of your fourth finger (pinkie)

How to Do It

❶ Chamber.

Start from your usual position, with your arms hanging at your sides and your right foot one step in front of your left foot. Close your left hand into a Karate fist, and make a *shuto* (sword) with your right hand.

Raise your right arm and cross it over the top of your left arm so that the "sword edge" of your right hand rests on your left shoulder.

❷ Chop.

Extend your right arm out in front of you. As you extend, twist your "sword hand" so that your right thumb knuckle ends up pointing directly to your left. At the same time, pull your left arm in toward your body to the chambered position just above your belt.

❸ Snap and shout.

When your arm is at full extension, your "sword hand" should be directly in line with your right shoulder. At the moment of full extension your left arm should be completely chambered at your left side. Give a loud *kiai!*

❹ Rechamber.

Repeat Step 1. Check that your left hand still makes a Karate fist, and your right hand still makes a good *shuto*.

Practice doing the Sword Hand Strike with a smooth snapping action similar to that of the Backfist Strike. Try the

Sword Hand from several different angles (imagine hitting a target at chest level, above chest level and at waist level). Then try it on your soft target.

Training Tip The Sword Hand is a very strong strike, and you can use it effectively from many angles.

Palm Heel Strike

Teisho
(tay show)

In the open-hand Palm Heel Strike, your hand looks like a bent Sword Hand. To form the Palm Heel, make a "sword hand" first and then push your wrist forward and pull your fingers back. Allow your fingers to relax a little, but keep your palm stiff. Your thumb should stay tucked along the side of your hand.

STRIKING SURFACE:
the area on your palm just above your wrist

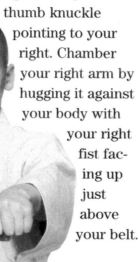

How to Do It

● Chamber.

Take your starting position and form Karate fists with both hands. Raise your left arm straight out in front of you to shoulder height, with your left thumb knuckle pointing to your right. Chamber your right arm by hugging it against your body with your right fist facing up just above your belt.

● Push and Pull.

Push your right arm straight out in front of you. As you push, open your right hand to form a Palm Heel as your arm is extending. Remember that your fingers should point up toward the ceiling and your palm should face away from you.

At the same time, pull your left fist in to the chambered position at your left side, just above your belt.

❸ Thrust and shout.

At the moment that your right arm is fully extended and your left fist is chambered, give a loud *kiai* and hold your position for a couple of seconds.

❹ Rechamber.

Back to Step 1. Your right arm should be tucked close to your side and your left arm should be extended—ready to strike again!

Just like the Sword Hand, the Palm Heel can be thrown at a target from many different angles. This is a very strong striking surface, since your Palm Heel is lined up with the bones in your forearm: the ulna and the radius.

Training Tip Unlike the Sword Hand and the Backfist strikes, the Palm Heel is usually done as a thrust.

Ridge Hand Strike

Haito

(high toh)

To form the "ridge hand," first make a "sword hand," then tuck your thumb under your palm. Keep your palm stiff and the back of your hand level with your wrist and forearm.

The arm-thrusting motion of this strike is the same as for the Palm Heel; only the hand position and striking surface differ.

STRIKING SURFACE: the triangular area formed between your wrist, index finger knuckle and thumb knuckle

How to Do It

● Chamber.

Begin with the same position as in Step 1 of the Palm Heel Strike. Raise your left arm straight out in front of you to shoulder height with your left thumb knuckle pointing to your right. Chamber your right arm.

● Push and Pull.

Push your right fist forward and pull your left arm in toward your body. As you push, form a "ridge hand" with your striking (right) hand.

● Thrust and shout.

Extend your right hand to the fullest, shout, and chamber your left arm. Your right hand should still be extended at about the level of your chin.

● Rechamber.

Return to the chamber position, as in Step 1: Your right fist pulled back, facing up, and snugly against your side. Your left fist is extended, face down.

Now move on to the Striking Power Drills on the next few pages. They'll help reinforce your strikng skills.

Training Tip The key to a good Ridge Hand is "rolling over" your striking hand just before you extend. With a smooth, rolling action, change your hand from a closed fist to an open Ridge Hand.

Striking Power Drill:

The News-Breaking Drill

Here's a good way to check the development of your punching power. You'll need to ask a parent or friend to be your helper.

Start with one sheet of newspaper at first, then move on to two or three and keep a daily record of your progress. Many years from now, when you can punch through a Sunday newspaper, you may make it into *The Guinness Book of World Records!*

(Note that the News-Breaking Drill can also be done with a Backfist Strike.)

1 Face your helper and position yourself about three feet away. Assume a Left Front Stance.

2 In very slow motion, do a Forefist Punch with your right hand and make sure that at its full extension your fist is still at least 12 inches away from your helper.

3 Ask your helper to hold up a sheet of old newspaper. The paper should be held both at the top and at the bottom.

4 Now throw your best and fastest Forefist Punch right at the middle of the newspaper. See if you can punch a hole clean through it without tearing the paper across.

Striking Power Drill:
Crack the Whip

Here's another way to make use of the daily newspaper in your Karate training. (Better be sure it's yesterday's paper!) Practice doing both right- and left-hand punches. You'll need a helper for this drill.

1 Take three sheets out of the newspaper and stack them. Fold the stack once lengthwise and once sideways. The stack should be approximately rectangular. Use masking tape or duct tape to tape around all the edges of the square so that it forms a "floating" soft target.

2 Have your helper stand in front of you and hold the target at the level of your nose. Assume a left Front Stance.

3 Ask your helper to let go of the target at any time. The exact time should be up to your helper, not you.

4 As the target falls to the level of your chest, hit it with a Forefist punch. Snap your punch and then quickly rechamber. Try to do this as fast as possible—as if you were cracking a whip. A strong *kiai* really helps.

Striking Power Drill:
The Jackhammer

The goal of this drill is to help you develop the power, speed and rhythm of a jackhammer—but without all the noise. The Jackhammer drill is also a way to review the proper hand formation for all six basic strikes.

Training Tip Work on your rhythm, and see if you can get your speed up to 60 punches in 60 seconds. Try practicing your *kiai* on the 10th strike of each technique.

1 Place your open left hand in front of you, and form a fist with your right hand.

2 Gently strike your left palm 10 times (while counting) with your right fist, using a Forefist Punch.

3 Now flip your right hand upside down and do Backfist Strikes on your left palm.

4 Continue by doing 10 Hammerfists, then 10 Sword Hands, 10 Palm Heels and finally 10 Ridge Hands, one right after the other.

Repeat the drill with your left hand striking your right. You can also vary the drill by switching from right to left with each different hand technique.

You shouldn't ever hit yourself hard enough to cause any pain. This drill is about learning control and form; it's not about force.

KARATE CHOP

Nice Guys Finish First

Actor Chuck Norris, the middleweight Karate champion of the late 1960s, is the only three-time member of the *Black Belt Magazine* Hall of Fame (Player, Instructor of the Year and Man of the Year). He has trained hundreds of students in Tang Soo Do, his special area of Karate study.

Norris usually plays a tough guy, but in real life he's known as a true gentleman.

Chuck Norris (standing, foreground), executing a move in the film Delta Force II: Columbian Connection.

Karate Courtesy:
Politeness and Respect

Learning to be courteous is one of the most important lessons in Karate. But it's not a lesson that can be learned from a lecture or by reading a chapter on courtesy in a book. If you stick with Karate, being courteous will become such a natural part of the way you live that you may have a hard time remembering whether you ever acted differently before!

All of the ancient martial arts place a great emphasis on courtesy. Most likely this is so because in Asian cultures there is a deeply rooted tradition of honoring elders. Respect for parents and grandparents, taught to every Asian child at a very early age, is echoed in the relationship of a

-WISE GUYS-

Karate begins and ends with courtesy.

—Gichin Funakoshi, Okinawan Karate master

Karate-ka to his older *sensei.*

Each martial art has several formalized ways to express courtesy. Respect for the training area is one of them; in most Asian *dojo,* students share the work of cleaning, and the *dojo* are usually spotless. You should keep your own training area clean and neat, remove your shoes before you enter it, and do not act foolish or childish while you are in it.

Bowing is another means of expressing respect. Technically, in most styles you don't have to bow to anyone but your teachers, but in fact most students also bow to any higher ranked students and to training partners.

Outward signs of respect such as bowing and keeping your training space neat are just a

KARATE CHOP

When Opposites Attract

The emphasis that most martial arts place on courtesy has roots in Asian philosophy. Many Asian people believe that life is made up of opposites. This concept is known as Yin and Yang: Yang represents people or things that are hard, strong and masculine. Yin represents people or things that are soft, yielding and feminine. Karate is both Yin and Yang because it combines fighting and toughness (Yang) with extreme courtesy and politeness (Yin).

small part of the picture. The bigger part must come from inside you: Karate courtesy means *having a sincere regard for the needs of others.* Karate masters know that discourteous people may be avoided or even feared, but they will never be respected. In Karate it is considered a sign of great strength for a person to be highly skilled in a fighting art, yet gentle and respectful to others.

Real masters know that Karate is more than just a training program. It's a way of life.

KICKS

The kicks of Karate are legendary for their speed, power and effectiveness in self-defense. The large muscles and bones in your legs give kicks their power. And because your legs are longer than your arms, kicking can be used from a greater distance than most hand techniques. That extra distance might allow you to execute your own offensive move while still remaining out of range of an opponent's strike.

In practical application, Karate kicking can be used not only for striking (an offensive move) but also for blocking (a defensive move). Whether it's a skipping side kick, a stomping kick or a sweeping kick, these moves add great versatility to the hand techniques you learned in the previous section.

There are many different kinds of kicks in Karate. The basic ones are the Front, Roundhouse, Back and Side kicks.

Learn one kick at a time, and learn it thoroughly. Practice the steps of the kick often, and use the Power Drills that follow the basic instructions. Be sure to practice each kick with both the right and left legs.

IN THIS SECTION:

Skills
Front Kick
Roundhouse Kick
Back Kick
Side Kick

Kicking Power Drills
Hot Foot Drill
The Alligator's Mouth
Bonkers Drill
Hip-Pop Drill

Roundhouse Kick, full extension.

Front Kick

Mae Geri
(my gary)

One of the most important kicks in Karate, the Front Kick is simple, quick and powerful. Since it requires only a minimum degree of flexibility, this kick is often one of the first skills taught to beginning students. Mastering the Front Kick helps you understand some of the moves needed for many advanced kicks.

The instructions will lead you through a right Front Kick.

STRIKING SURFACE: the ball of your foot (the underside of the front of your foot)

How to Do It

❶ Balance your stance.
Stand with both feet flat on the ground, shoulder-width apart, with your toes pointing straight forward. Place your left foot about one normal step in front of you for better balance. Keep your back straight and your arms close to your body but not tight against you. Your left arm should be held slightly higher than the right, ready to block or grab.

❷ Chamber.
Raise your right knee so that your right thigh is parallel to the floor. This action is like putting your foot up on a chair to tie your shoe. Keep your right foot close to your left leg, and hold your right foot up as though you were trying to hold a soccer ball on top of it. Keep your back straight and hold your arms as you did in Step 1.

❸ Extend.

Extend your right leg straight out in front of you so that your foot is waist-high. Make sure your toes are still pulled back, but push your foot forward so that the ball of your foot is aimed at the target. Check that your back is still straight and your arms held close to the body. Your left foot should remain as it was in Step 1, pointing forward.

❹ Rechamber.

Pull your right foot back so that you end up in the same position for Step 2, the chamber step. Your right thigh should be parallel to the floor.

Training Tip Here's where the flexibility you develop in your warm-up could really pay off. For a great Front Kick, raise the knee of your kicking leg up as high as you can—if possible, your knee should point at the target you are kicking.

❺ Resume balanced stance.

Place your right foot on the floor. You're back to Step 1. Check that your back is straight and your balance is solid.

Practice each step of the Front Kick separately at first, then blend them into one smooth sequence. As you get the feel of the kick, speed it up so that it snaps out. Practice that snapping action against your soft target, and remember to give a *kiai*.

Roundhouse Kick

Mawashi Geri
(mah wah shee gary)

Another very basic Karate kick, the Roundhouse comes at a target from the side. Since this kick requires a lot of flexibility, you should not try to kick above waist height unless you're well stretched. The key to a great Roundhouse is proper timing of the pivot. To pivot, shift your weight to the ball of your non-kicking foot; then turn the heel of that foot into the direction of the kick.

STRIKING SURFACE: either the ball of your foot or the instep (which is the top of the front of your foot)

How to Do It

1 Balance your stance. Start in the same position as you did for the Front Kick: feet shoulder-width apart, left foot one step forward, arms close to your body.

2 Chamber. Raise your right knee up to your side (not to the front), with your foot tucked in against your rear end.

❸ Knee up.

Thrust your knee forward and point it directly at the target. At the same time pivot your left foot to your left so that your toes point to the side. Keep your hands in close to your chest.

Training Tip Even though you may be inclined to focus all your attention on accurately hitting the target, don't forget to put your foot down in a totally controlled manner after completing a kick. Otherwise, you might lose your balance.

❹ Extend.

Extend your foot outward and point the ball of your foot at the target. Impact will occur when your leg is fully extended. Your pivot foot (the left) should stop turning at the instant your right foot reaches full extension.

❺ Rechamber.

Pull the heel of your kicking foot back to your rear end, but leave your kicking knee pointed at the target as in step 3.

❻ Resume balanced stance.

Return the kicking leg to the floor either in front of you or behind you.

Practice each step of the Roundhouse Kick separately at first, then blend them into one smooth sequence. As you get the feel of the kick, speed it up so that it really snaps out. Practice that snapping action against your soft target and remember to give a loud *kiai*.

Back Kick

Ushiro Geri
(ooh shee roh gary)

If you've ever seen a movie in which a mule or horse uses its rear legs to kick backward and knock a door off its hinges or blast through a wooden fence, you've seen the power of a Back Kick.

Unlike a mule kick, though, the Karate Back Kick uses one leg at a time. The kick should have a powerful thrust or a whiplike snap. The instructions here are for a right-leg Back Kick.

STRIKING SURFACE: either the "blade" (outer edge) or the heel of your foot

How to Do It

❶ Balance your stance.
Stand with your feet shoulder-width apart. Then move your right foot one step backward. Turn your head to the right in order to look behind you.

❷ Chamber.
Raise your right leg up so that your right knee is about as high as your belt; tuck your right foot in with your right heel pointing behind you.

3 Extend.

Push your right leg out behind you until it's completely straight. Your foot should be positioned like a blade edge, and it should be about as high as your belt.

4 Rechamber.

Pull your right leg back toward you so that your right knee swings up in front of you, almost like a Front Kick chamber. Try to keep your back straight.

Training Tip Keep your eyes on your target when you're using the Back Kick.

5 Resume balanced stance.

Back to Step 1. Your eyes should still be looking in the same direction as your kick.

Now try a left-leg Back Kick. When you practice with a soft target, you'll find that accuracy is quite a challenge in a Back Kick.

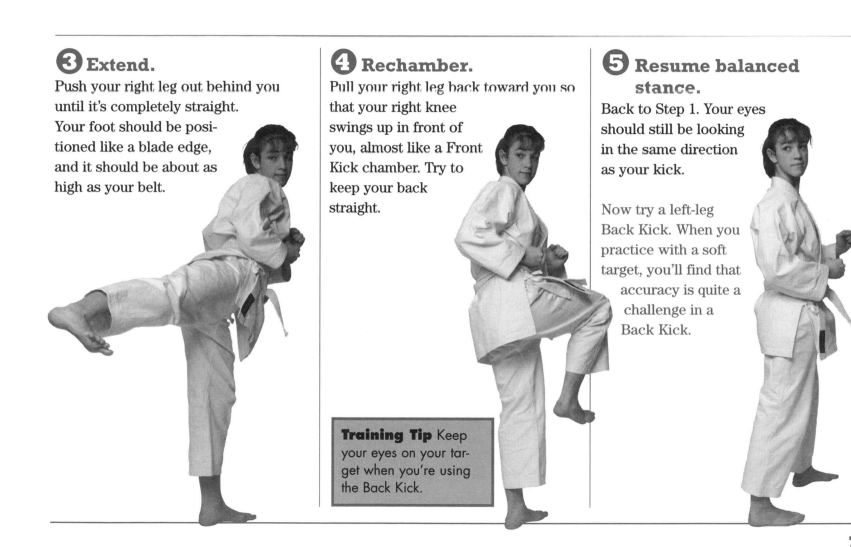

Side Kick

Yoko Geri
(yoh koh gary)

The Side Kick is very powerful and useful for kicking from greater distances. As in the Roundhouse, the thrusting action of the kicking leg must be perfectly timed with the pivot of the support foot.

The Side Kick is one of the most powerful movements in Karate and Tae Kwon Do.

STRIKING SURFACE: the blade or the heel of your foot

How to Do It

❶ Balance your stance.

Stand with your feet shoulder-width apart and your toes pointing forward. Make Karate fists with both hands, and bring your arms up close to your chest. The exact position of your arms is not critical, but keeping them close to your body helps you remain balanced during the kick.

❷ Chamber.

Raise your right knee so that your right thigh is parallel to the floor, as if you were putting your foot up on a chair to tie your shoe. Keep your right knee close to your left leg, and hold your right foot up as if you were trying to hold a soccer ball on top of it. Keep your back straight and maintain your arm position from Step 1.

❸ Pivot.

Turn your head and look to your right. Raise your right foot until your leg is parallel with the floor. Pivot on your left foot to the left until your toes are pointing directly opposite the direction in which you're looking.

Training Tip Some styles of Karate use the toe knuckles as a striking surface for kicks, but most don't because toe injuries can result. Generally, you should use the strong parts of your foot, such as the ball or the edge, for thrusting kicks.

❹ Extend.

Push your right heel out to your right side until your right leg is completely straight. Try to keep your body upright without leaning: your arms should remain close to your body.

The better stretched you are, the higher you will be able to kick; for now, kick only as high as your belt.

❺ Rechamber.

Pull your right leg back into the chamber position (as in Step 2) and turn your left foot back to its original position, toes pointing forward.

❻ Resume balanced stance.

Back to Step 1. If you lost your balance and wobbled during the pivot, take a deep breath, rest for a moment, focus on your balance and try again.

Try the Side Kick using your soft target. It's a tough kick to learn, so don't worry about your speed; instead, concentrate on your accuracy.

Kicking Power Drill:
Hot Foot Drill

These Kicking Power Drills will super-train the muscles of your legs. They are a great way to get extra practice for the parts that make up a kick, like chambering and extending; they will also start you working on your timing, an important skill you will need someday when you're up against a moving target.

1 Place your feet shoulder-width apart. Be sure that your toes are pointing straight forward and that your back is straight. Place your hands palms down at waist level, with your left hand resting lightly on top of your right hand. Keep your chin up and away from your chest, and look forward.

2 With a quick and snappy movement (as if you were marching in a parade), pull your right knee up until it meets your right hand. Don't allow your hands to move below your waist, and keep your back straight and your chin up. Breathe out through your mouth when your knee hits your hands. A good strong *kiai* will help you breathe better.

3 The moment your knee hits your hand, quickly drop your leg and place your foot back flat on the floor. Avoid smashing your heel onto the floor.

Repeat with the other leg, and continue to alternate—right, left, right, and so on. You might ask a friend to count in Japanese or Korean for this drill. (See page 35 to learn how.)

Kicking Power Drill:
The Alligator's Mouth

Your goal in this drill is to pull your foot back from your target before the alligator's jaws can "bite" your foot. The drill will help develop the muscles that allow you to do a fast kick retraction (pulling your foot back from a target).

1 Ask your helper to kneel down on one leg and open his or her arms widely as shown in the photograph. Prepare to do a Front Kick so that your foot will go between your helper's extended arms.

2 Pull your right knee up to the chamber position. Keep your back straight, and don't allow your foot to dangle. Always keep your bottom foot pointed at the target.

3 Extend your leg directly between your helper's arms.

4 Quickly pull your foot out from the alligator's "jaws" before he can shut them on your foot.

Remember your balance, foot position and posture. Repeat the exercise many times. As you practice, you should find that you beat the alligator more times than he can bite your leg!

83

Kicking Power Drill:
Bonkers Drill

This drill requires help from a friend or family member and the use of a "bonking" device. Cardboard wrapping paper tubes, lightweight hollow safety baseball bats or the plastic tubes used in golf bags (about 36 inches long and usually available at sports stores) all make good "bonkers."

1 Place your feet shoulder-width apart. Point your toes straight forward and keep your back straight. Place your hands, palms down, at waist level. Keep your chin up and away from your chest, and look forward. Ask your helper to hold the bonker about ankle high and about two feet in front of your ankles.

Training Tip Try to have fun with this drill, but don't go "bonkers" yourself! Your helper should try to bonk you quickly but not too hard. At the beginning, ask your helper to keep pace with you and not to go so fast that you never succeed in beating the bonker.

2 Have your helper shout "go" or count "one" and then try to bonk (slap) your ankle with the bonker before you can pull your knee up and out of the way. Your job is to pull your knee up so fast that your helper can't hit your ankle. If he or she misses your ankle, the bonker will hit your other leg and make a loud "bonk."

3 After the bonker is moved back away from you, place your leg back down and repeat the movement. Practice with each leg (one at a time) and repeat the drill many times.

Kicking Power Drill:
Hip-Pop Drill

Here's a great way to help you practice placing your foot properly on a target during a Front Kick. You'll need an empty two-liter plastic soda bottle without its cap. You'll also need a helper. The plastic bottle you will be kicking is soft enough so that it won't hurt your foot, yet firm enough for you to feel the way your foot makes contact with the bottle when it "squooshes."

1 Place your feet shoulder-width apart and put your right foot about 24 inches behind your left into a Front Stance. Make sure that your toes are pointing straight forward toward your target and that your back is straight. Have your helper hold the soda bottle at about the height of your belly button. Your helper should hold the bottle tightly in both hands.

Training Tip If the plastic bottle cracks or breaks, immediately replace it with a new bottle. Don't forget to recycle the bottle when you're done!

2 Pull your right knee up to the chamber position as shown. Keep your back straight and don't allow your foot to dangle. Keep your eyes on the target.

3 Extend your right leg out quickly and hit the bottle with the ball of your foot.

4 Pull your foot back quickly into the chamber position. Remember to keep your back straight and think about your balance.

5 Return your foot to the floor and prepare to kick again.

Karate Courage:

Making Good Choices

All of us have felt fear or worry in our lives. Fear is a natural response to a scary situation, and feeling afraid is a normal human emotion. In fact, sometimes fear is good for us: it helps us react quickly in a dangerous situation, such as a fire or an oncoming car.

But it's important not to let fear hold us back from enjoying life and from being our best. Too much fear in our daily lives can be a source of great unhappiness. Yet there is something we can do about it.

–WISE GUYS–

**Knowing others is intelligence;
Knowing yourself is true wisdom.
Mastering others is strength;
Mastering yourself is true power.**

—Lao-tzu, Chinese philosopher

Karate students and teachers believe that fear can be decreased by building courage. Both fear and courage arise from within you; they are not given to you by anyone or anything. It's up to you to determine which will be stronger. In Karate you will learn new ways to build courage. For example, you might be asked to demonstrate a skill in front of someone who is at a higher level of training than yourself. Students develop Karate courage as they

"Karate taught me that it's OK to be afraid; it's what you do with your fear that matters." —Stephanie, age 13

learn each new skill, work through the difficulties of each rank and face each new challenge successfully.

If you join a *dojo,* you might be called on to lead the class through exercises by counting, or you might participate in games in which you must outwit an opponent with your skill. Even shouting, which to an outsider might seem like just a lot of noise, is a way of developing the courage to express yourself.

If you think about courage and practice doing courageous things, you can strengthen your courage so it will be there to help you when you do feel fear; you'll just look back on all of the brave things you've already done and the suc-

cesses you've had, and you'll know that you can succeed again.

Karate students also believe that courage can be strengthened by changing the way they think— and the best way to think is positively. To do this, just make a mental image of the best possible outcome of a fearful situation instead of the worst one.

Positive thinking can be a big help in training, too. The best way to learn a new Karate skill is to think about yourself doing it perfectly, even before you try it. It might not work right away, but if you keep that positive picture in your mind, sooner or later your real action will come close to matching the picture you have been imagining.

Positive thinking applies to life outside Karate, too. Suppose you're asked to stand up in front of your classmates in school and give a speech. If you start out thinking that you're just a bad speaker and that no one wants to listen to you, fear will creep into your mind and chances are the speech will go poorly.

Instead, make a positive mental picture of yourself giving a great speech; imagine your teacher being impressed by how well you did and your friends giving you big high fives for pulling it off. At the very least, positive thinking may help you find the courage to give the speech your best effort; and giving your best is what life is all about.

BLOCKS

Karate is an art of self-defense, and many experts feel that blocking is a very important part of the discipline. Karate masters believe that becoming good at blocking makes a Karate-ka feel confident, calm and ever prepared. A Karate-ka who blocks well can make himself "unavailable" to an opponent. In fact, it's said that a good blocker can almost disappear!

Think of blocking as a means of deflecting a strike by placing something in its way. Karate-ka can block with both their arms and legs—though leg blocks are more advanced.

The first principle of blocking is to avoid a strike, and the best way to do that is to get out of the way in a hurry. As you practice blocking skills and drills, you'll increase the speed of your reflexes and decrease the amount of time it would take you to react to a strike.

The second principle of blocking is deflection, or sending power in a new direction. A block that deflects power is called a receptive block. With practice, you'll learn how you could use an opponent's power against him or, at the very least, render his strike less powerful. Think of your blocking arm or leg as a broom that could sweep away an opponent's strikes, not as a car bumper that would absorb the shock of a direct crash.

IN THIS SECTION:

Skills
High Block
Low Block
Inside Middle Block
Outside Middle Block

Blocking Power Drills
 The Magic Door
 New Kid on the Block
 The "Blockhead"
  Drill

A High Block in Front Stance.

High Block

Age Uke
(ah gay ooh kay)

The High Block is used to defend the area from your shoulders to the top of your head. The goal of the High Block is to use your blocking arm to deflect a strike by sweeping it away. A correctly done High Block may give you a chance to escape an opponent, prevent further strikes, or clear the way for *you* to use a strike or kick.

The instructions are for a left-handed block, but remember to practice all the blocks with both hands.

How to Do It

❶ Cross your arms.

Make fists with both hands. Cross your arms in front of you so that your left forearm is across your belly and your right arm is on top of your left.

Your right elbow should be positioned just above your left forearm, and the knuckle of your right thumb should be touching your left shoulder. The knuckle of your left fist should be aiming forward in front of your face. Hold your arms close to your body.

❷ Push and pull.

Pull your right elbow down while twisting your right forearm; feel the arm slide against your right side. Your right fist should be turning so that your thumb moves away from you. At the same time, push your left arm upward, twisting your left fist so that the knuckle of your thumb moves toward you. Your left arm should pass six to eight inches in front of your face, and your left fist should *always* be above your left elbow.

③ Snap and shout.

Keep pulling your right elbow back while twisting that arm until your right fist is pressed against your right side. Keep your right shoulder relaxed and your right elbow close to you. At the same time, push your left arm upward until your left fist is four to five inches above and in front of your head. As you reach completion of the block, snap your wrists and give a *kiai*.

When your High Block is completed, your left elbow should end up to the left of your head at about eye level. The knuckle of your left thumb should be pointing toward the floor. Both left and right wrists should be straight.

Training Tip When you practice blocks, focus on making smooth, circular movements with your arms. Try not to make your blocks rigid or abrupt.

KARATE CHOP

Clean Sweep

In many *dojo* it's customary for students to sweep or wipe the floor clean after training sessions. This is a tradition drawn from the Japanese philosophy called Zen. Cleaning the floor symbolizes the wiping away of delusions or trivial ideas from students' minds.

Low Block

Gedan Barai
(gay dahn bah rye)

The Low Block can be used to deflect blows (usually kicks) aimed toward the lower region of your body from your belly to your knees. This block may be broken down into three steps that are very similar to the steps of the High Block.

The instructions show you a left-handed Low Block.

Training Tip When blocking, a true Karate master uses just the right amount of energy needed to deflect an attack and no more. That extra bit of energy might be required for the next move!

How to Do It

❶ Cross your arms.

Cross your arms against your chest so that your right arm is across your belly, your right fist is closed, and your thumb knuckle is close to your left side. Your left arm should be crossed over the top of your right arm so that your left elbow is resting on your right forearm, your left fist closed, and your left thumb knuckle is pointing toward your front. Inhale through your nose.

❷ Push and pull.

Push your left arm down so that it sweeps one to two inches in front of your chest and belly while twisting your wrist so that your thumb knuckle faces to your right. Your left arm should stop just above your left thigh. At the same time, pull your right arm in to your right side to the chambered position. Exhale through your mouth as you block.

③ Snap and shout.

Finish the block with a brisk snap, a *kiai* and a full exhale.

Now try a right-handed Low Block.

Patching It Up

Lots of Karate-ka like to collect colorful embroi-dered martial arts patches. These patches come in all shapes, sizes, and designs: some have martial arts words or initials of organizations; some are based on the flags of foreign countries; and some depict animals such as tigers or dragons.

Most Karate schools and organizations have rules about what kind of patches their members can wear, and many of them have their own special patches. A student would wear such a patch on the jacket of his *gi*, just over his heart, as a symbol of loyalty to that organization.

You can buy patches in martial arts supply stores. If you're a beginner training at home, there's no reason why you can't put a cool patch on the sweatshirt or T-shirt you wear to train.

Inside Middle Block

Uchi Ude Uke
(ooh chee ooh day ooh kay)

This block is used to protect the area from your shoulders to your ribs. It follows the same sequence of steps as the High Block, but it has different beginning and ending positions.

These directions explain a right Inside Middle Block.

Training Tip
The Inside Middle Block uses a motion similar to throwing a Frisbee from waist level.

How to Do It

1 Cross your arms.
Place your left arm across the front of your body so that your left thumb knuckle touches your right shoulder. Cross your right arm in front of you and under your left arm so that your elbows are nearly touching. The thumb knuckle of your right fist should be near your right side, just under your armpit. Keep your shoulders relaxed.

2 Sweep and pull.
Sweep your right arm out in front of you so that your right fist stops in front of your right shoulder. The crook of your right arm should be bent at about 45 degrees. Your right elbow should be a few inches in front of your right ribs. Twist your fist as it swings out so that your right thumb knuckle ends up pointing to your right.

At the same time, pull your left arm in toward the chambered position.

❸ Snap and shout.

Your arms should move together and you should feel a "snap" when your arms stop. At the moment that your right arm stops and your left arm is completely chambered, give a loud *kiai*.

Once you've worked on your right-handed Inside Middle Block, practice doing it with your left hand.

KARATE CHOP

Flash Dancers

The person who coordinates the fight scenes in a movie or TV show is called a fight choreographer. That title reminds us that when done properly the martial arts have graceful, fluid movements similar to dancing. The classic film *The Karate Kid* (1984), for instance, was choreographed by Pat Johnson, who was a student of Chuck Norris and a great Karate champion himself.

If you see *The Karate Kid,* watch for the scene in which Daniel wins the final match of a tournament by using a Jumping Front Kick. But note that holding your arms out like wings is *not* required for the kick.

Ralph Macchio (at left) and Pat Morita, in The Karate Kid.

Outside Middle Block

Soto Ude Uke
(soe toe ooh day ooh kay)

The Outside Middle Block protects the same area as the Inside Middle block, but it's a much stronger move.

Unlike the other three basic blocks, this one does not involve crossing your arms in front of you. Instead, each fist starts on its own side of your body.

Training Tip The action of the Outside Middle Block is similar to a baseball player pitching a curve ball over home plate.

How to Do It

● Chamber.

Raise your left arm up to shoulder height with your left thumb knuckle pointing to your right. Raise your right arm up so that your right fist almost touches your right ear. Your right elbow should be as high as your ear and pointing to your right.

● Sweep and pull.

Sweep your right arm down in front of you with a twisting motion so that your right fist stops directly in front of your chin but a few inches below it. Your right thumb knuckle should be facing right, and the crook of your elbow should form an angle of 45 degrees. Your right elbow should be a few inches in front of your chest.

At the same time, pull your left arm in toward your body.

3 Snap and shout.

Snap your block into full extension, and chamber your left arm tightly against you. Give a loud *kiai*. The extension, the chamber and the *kiai* should all happen at the same time.

As you practice the Outside Middle Block, focus on keeping the sweeping motion of your right arm smooth. Then switch to a left-handed Outside Middle Block.

Now move on to the Blocking Power Drills. They'll help you improve your blocking skills, your reflexes and your alertness.

—WISE GUYS—

In walking, just walk. In sitting, just sit. Above all, don't wobble.

—Yun-men

Blocking Power Drill:
The Magic Door

This drill is a great way to quicken the reflexes you'll need in order to avoid a strike.

Use a lightweight soft tube like the one used for the Bonkers Drill (see page 84.) The cardboard tube from a roll of wrapping paper is the best "bonker."

Ask a friend or family member to be your helper.

1 Stand in front of your helper with your chest facing him and your arms up, as if a robber just told you to "stick 'em up."

2 Your helper will then raise the tube above his head and slowly lower it down at your head as if he were chopping wood.

3 Before the tube comes down on your head, pivot on your left foot and step back with your right foot. Make believe your body is a magic door that has just sprung open on its hinges after somebody said the magic words. Your body should end up sideways, with both feet pointing in the same direction as your chest, but your eyes should never leave the approaching strike.

The tube should pass down a few inches in front of you, without touching you, all the way to the floor.

Repeat the drill and move your other foot back. Increase your speed as you get the hang of it.

Training Tip Think of the smooth, even movement of an opening door. Try to make your body move the same way.

KARATE CHOP

The King of Karate Comedy

The most famous action film star in the world is Hong Kong native Jackie Chan. Chan invented a new movie genre called the Kung Fu comedy, which combined slapstick comic antics with exciting and theatrical martial arts scenes. Inspired by great comedians such as Charlie Chaplin and Buster Keaton, he performed some of the funniest and scariest stunts ever, including rolling down a mountain inside a beach ball.

Chan writes, produces and directs many of his films himself. He's also a major pop music singer and performs many of his films' theme songs, too.

Film star Jackie Chan.

Blocking Power Drill:
New Kid on the Block

This is a great drill for students who are new to Karate blocking; it incorporates all four basic blocks and gets you used to choosing which one of them to use. You will need a "bonker" like the one described in the Bonkers Drill (see page 84) as well as a helper.

1 Stand with your feet shoulder-width apart and one foot slightly in front of the other. Hold your arms in front of you and make good Karate fists.

2 Ask your helper to slowly swing the bonker toward your body. It's your helper's choice—he can swing the bonker from the right or from the left, in any of these directions:

• straight down toward your head

• straight forward toward your stomach

• sideways toward your mid-side

• sideways toward your hips

3 It's your job to block the bonker with the appropriate basic block. For example, if the bonker is coming in toward your left hip, use your left-handed Low Block.

After you try this drill for a while, you will figure out the correct block for each approach—it's the one that works!

Training Tip This drill helps you practice alertness and anticipation so you get used to being ready for anything.

4 The moment you do the block, give a loud *kiai*. Your partner should immediately switch the direction of the bonker, requiring you to use a new block.

Ask your partner to vary the direction of the bonker to include all the ways listed on the facing page. Practice slowly at first, then speed it up. Using the right block takes quick thinking.

KARATE CHOP

Beam Me Up, Sensei

Fans of martial arts and also the TV show *Star Trek* may remember an episode called "Charlie X," which included a Judo scene.

The show featured the "Kirk Maneuver," done by lacing your fingers together and swinging both fists as one. Trekkies take heart: in real life William Shatner, who played Captain Kirk, is a black belt in Kenpo.

Blocking Power Drill:
The "Blockhead" Drill

Have you ever been the victim of name-calling at school? Almost every kid has, and it can hurt more than a punch or a kick. This drill can help you learn how to keep your cool when you're up against a name-caller. Using the concept of receptive blocking, it shows you how to create "verbal blocks" that can render words powerless.

You'll need a soft tube like the one described on page 84. For this drill, imagine that the tube is a great sword like those used to dub medieval knights.

You'll also need a helper, and for this drill it might be best to ask an adult . . . a friend might not understand what's going on.

1 Begin as you did in the Magic Door drill, standing in front of your helper with your arms raised in a "stick 'em up" position. Ask your mom or dad to raise the tube and slowly bring it down toward your head.

2 Your helper must now call you either a kind name or a mean one while lowering the tube.

3 If your helper says something nice like "What a smart kid," you must stay put and smile as you get gently "dubbed" on the head or shoulder like a knight.

4 If your helper says something mean—like "Hey, Blockhead"— then do a quick body pivot just as you did in the Magic Door drill. Allow the bonker (like a negative word) to pass by without touching you.

> **Training Tip** When somebody calls you a mean name, it can be pretty difficult to ignore. Since they don't know a better way, most kids react to name-calling by getting angry. But anger can get you into trouble, and it usually doesn't stop the name-calling.

5 Once the tube passes by you, return to center, smile, and say "That's interesting" or "You can believe whatever you want."

You might assist your helper by revealing some of the names that you or your friends at school have been called. Then you and your helper can work on your verbal blocks—the things to say to yourself or others in order to deflect the power of name-calling.

The point of this drill is that nobody has the power to make you angry but yourself. When people call you a name, all they are doing is vibrating your eardrum with a sound. You give words power or take power away by the meaning you attach to them. And learning to block and deflect foolish words will enable you to get on with the important things in your life!

KARATE CHOP

Balancing Act

Great martial artists train hard, but they also strive for balance in their lives. Super-athelete Kathy Long, a black belt in Karate, Kung Fu and Aikido, was asked in an interview if there was room in her life for anything else. Sure, she answered: there's chocolate chip cookies, playing the guitar and her golden retriever named Abbey.

Karate Confidence:
Believing in Yourself

Building Karate confidence requires you to start thinking about yourself in new ways. If you have confidence, you won't feel the need to get angry with yourself or blame somebody else when you are faced with a problem. You will simply believe you can find a way to solve the problem—and most times you will.

Karate masters believe that confidence can be strengthened by experiencing many successes. A Karate-ka is encouraged to set his or her own goals, and every goal reached represents a success. Students who have made it through beginner level have built up a great store of successes. They are becoming confident people.

Every time you master a new skill, or even one step of a skill, you add to your own store of confidence-building successes. When you first practice the Side Kick, for instance, you might feel as if there is *no way* you will ever be able to pivot on one foot without losing your balance. If you stick with it, though, you *will* master it: another success to add to your store. Almost every training session includes at least one success, no matter how small.

Confidence Builders

Here are some good habits that can help build Karate confidence during your own training:

1 Practice controlling your strikes and kicks until you can stop them within one inch of your soft target. This helps you to feel confident that you have control over your surroundings.

2 When you get pretty good at a skill, do it in front of a friend or

"I think everyone should take Karate so they can feel good like me." —Kristen, age 5

-WISE GUYS-

I t is good to have an end to journey toward; but it is the journey that matters, in the end.

—Ursula K. Le Guin, American writer

debate at school; or you might find yourself having to run the last lap of a relay race when your team is behind. Maybe you'll call on your Karate confidence when a whole group of your friends try to talk you into doing something you don't want to do.

Karate confidence means inner strength, and if you stick with your training you'll develop the confidence to get stronger every day.

a family member. Remember, this is not about showing off; it's about having the confidence to perform well when someone is watching.

3 Practice your *kiai* a lot. The extra burst of energy you get from the *kiai*

is a great confidence builder.

Confidence is the most important Karate value of all, and before long you will encounter situations outside your training in which you can use it: maybe you'll be called upon to participate in a

The Greeting People Drill

How to Do It

The Greeting People drill is a "made in the USA" version of the bow that Karate students practice in Asian countries. It's a very simple drill, but it has something to teach you about building confidence on a very basic level—after all, it often takes confidence to look someone in the eye and express yourself directly.

1 Begin by asking a parent or a brother or sister to help. Stand right in front of your partner and look directly into his or her eyes. Put out your right hand, and when your partner takes it to shake, say:

"Hi, my name is John (use your own name), what's yours?"

Your partner should then reply with his or her own name. Let's say it's your sister Alison. You then answer:

"I'm pleased to meet you, Alison."

2 While you're speaking, look directly into your partner's eyes; make your handshake firm without squeezing too hard, and speak clearly.

Later, do the greeting drill with other members of your family and then with other relatives or friends. With practice, you will develop the confidence to always look others in the eye when you meet them; on a larger scale, you will learn to express yourself to others.

-PART 3-
GOING FURTHER

Choosing a *Dojo* and a *Sensei*

efore you choose a Karate school and an instructor, talk to people with experience and ask plenty of questions. Talk to kids and their parents, to relatives, neighbors and friends—anyone who might have at least six months' experience with a martial arts school. You'll find that most people who are into Karate are more than glad to talk about it.

It's best to choose a school that's not more than 20 or 30 minutes from your home; classes are frequent and a longer trip could be a burden.

Once you've narrowed down the choices, visit each school at least three times (one time unannounced.) Bring your own list of questions, including some tough

ones, and see if your prospective teachers will pass the test! Here's a sample list:

What are the ages of students in a class? (Kids under 10 should be in classes with kids: kids over 10 can train with adults with their parents' approval.)

How often would your class be held? (You need at least two classes a week.)

How long is the class? (Classes should be a minimum of 30 to 45 minutes long for kids.)

Do the instructors have experience teaching kids? (They should.)

Are parents allowed to watch the whole class? (They should be.)

Is competition a focus of the school? (You can advance far in Karate without ever competing in tournaments, but if you are interested in competing, you'll need a school that will help you get started.)

Finally, be sure you get to meet the instructor who will be leading

"Karate has taught me to respect my teachers and my parents." —Taylor, age 9

the particular class you enroll in. The instructor should be someone with a personality strong enough to inspire you but not scare you: a good *sensei* offers his students motivation without intimidation.

What you will have to pay for Karate classes varies a lot. Most full-service schools (open five or six days a week) charge between $50 and $80 per month. Don't be surprised if a school won't tell you about cost over the phone: the representative may feel that you would not understand the reason for their prices unless you come to see the *dojo* for yourself. Remember that a school is also likely to charge for rank promotions (most schools have rank promotions every two to four

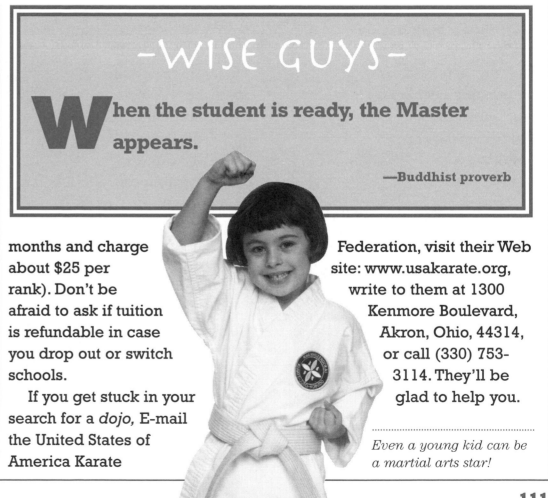

—WISE GUYS—

When the student is ready, the Master appears.

—Buddhist proverb

months and charge about $25 per rank). Don't be afraid to ask if tuition is refundable in case you drop out or switch schools.

If you get stuck in your search for a *dojo,* E-mail the United States of America Karate

Federation, visit their Web site: www.usakarate.org, write to them at 1300 Kenmore Boulevard, Akron, Ohio, 44314, or call (330) 753-3114. They'll be glad to help you.

Even a young kid can be a martial arts star!

Looking Ahead to Advanced Karate

Do you want to take a look beyond the basics? If you do decide to make a commitment to Karate and join a *dojo,* there's a whole lot more to learn.

One thing, though . . . even if you make it to black belt or further, you will *never* really stop practicing the basics. You will encounter students at high levels who still practice their Forefist Punches and Front Kicks regularly. The basic skills you have learned in *The Kids' Karate Book* will always be the core of your training, even though you will learn to do those skills with more refined form, faster and more accurately. In other words, you're already doing much of what an advanced Karate-ka does!

As an advanced student you will learn a great many new strikes, kicks and blocks, a few of which are illustrated here. Most of these advanced movements build on the basic skills, such as chambering and pivoting, that you have already begun to practice.

There are two very important skills that will be totally new to you as an advanced student: *forms* and *sparring.*

Jumping Front Kick chamber position.

Knife Hand Strike in a Right Back Stance, a movement very common in kata.

Karate competitions emphasize quick thinking and concentrated energy; a typical bout lasts only two or three minutes.

Forms

Forms, called *kata* (pronounced *kah tah*) in Japanese and *hyung* (*hee young*) in Korean, are a series of formal movements strung together in an unbroken chain. Each style of Karate has a number of forms, and each form has a name. Sometimes done slowly and sometimes quickly, forms look like choreographed dances; embedded within them, though, are effective self-defense techniques known only to the most experienced masters.

Outside Crescent Kick, an acrobatic kick requiring great flexibility.

Sparring

As an advanced student, you will also learn to *spar.* Sparring, called *kumite* (*koo mee tay*) in Japanese and *daeryon* (*dye ree on*) in Korean, means trying your skills against an opponent. At first, students spar with no contact at all. Much later, they learn how to execute moves with very light contact.

Sparring is carefully controlled fighting that is done only with proper gear and under the supervision of a *sensei.*

This is the first movement of a kata *called* Heian Nidan. *In Japanese,* Heian *refers to a peaceful nature.*

The *Dojo* Bookshelf:
More Books About Karate and the Martial Arts

Children and the Martial Arts: An Aikido Point of View, by Gaku Momma. North Atlantic Books, Berkeley, California, 1993.

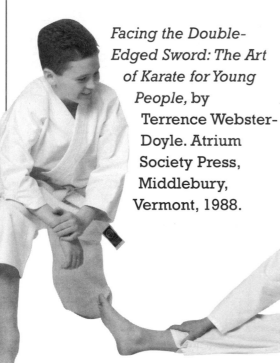

Facing the Double-Edged Sword: The Art of Karate for Young People, by Terrence Webster-Doyle. Atrium Society Press, Middlebury, Vermont, 1988.

Karate Techniques and Tactics for Kids, by Patrick M. Hickey. Human Kinetics Publishers, Champaign, Illinois, 1997.

Martial Arts for Kids, by Richard Devins and Norman Sandler. Weatherhill, Inc., New York, 1997.

The Tiger's Eye, The Bird's Fist: A Beginner's Guide to the Martial Arts, by Louise Rafkin. Little, Brown & Company, New York, 1997.

A Parent's Guide to Martial Arts, by Deborah Fritsch and Ruth Hunter. Turtle Press, New York, 1998.

The Young Martial Arts Enthusiast, by David Mitchell. DK Publishing, Inc., New York, 1997.

Want to learn more about Karate? Talk to other Karate-ka; rent Karate movies; read Karate books and magazines; and attend Karate competitions. Karate students are students for life.